The E

MW01034765

"...an opinionated little compendium."
~ New York Times

"...irresistible little guide."
~ Chicago Tribune

"an elegant, small guide..."
~ Minneapolis Star Tribune

"Makes dining easy and enjoyable."
~ Toronto Sun

"...a terrific primer for first-time visitors."
~ Houston Chronicle

*"...opening up the world of good eating with their
innovative paperback series."*
~ Salt Lake Tribune

"...travelers who know their cervelle *(brains) from*
cervelle de canut *(herbed cheese spread)."*
~ USA Today

"It's written as if a friend were talking to you."
~ Celebrity Chef Tyler Florence

"...artfully designed – the perfect gift."
~ Milwaukee Journal Sentinel

*"A dietary dictionary to help you decipher
'ropa vieja' as shredded beef, not old clothes!"*
~ Caribbean Travel & Life

ABOUT THE AUTHOR

Andy Herbach is a lawyer and resides in Milwaukee, Wisconsin. He is the author of *Eating and Drinking in Paris* and *Eating and Drinking in Italy*.

Andy is also the author of several books published by Open Road, including *Best of Paris*, *Best of Provence and the French Riviera*, and *Best of Spain*.

You can e-mail comments, additions and corrections to eatndrink@aol.com.

UPDATES
Updates to this guide can be found at www.eatndrink.com.

ACKNOWLEDGMENTS

Marian Olson (when she could be dragged away from the *bodegas*) is the best editor ever.

Thanks to Karl Raaum for all his help.

Portions of this book were previously published in *Eating & Drinking in Spain* and *Eating & Drinking in Latin America* by Andy Herbach and Michael Dillon.

EATING AND DRINKING IN

Spain
and Portugal

Spanish Menu Translator
Portuguese Menu Translator
Restaurant Guide

Andy Herbach

OPEN ROAD PUBLISHING

OPEN ROAD PUBLISHING

Your passport to the perfect trip!

Open Road Publishing
P.O. Box 284
Cold Spring Harbor, NY 11724

www.openroadguides.com

Library of Congress Control Number: 2011931839
ISBN-10: 1593601514
ISBN-13: 9781593601515

EATING AND DRINKING IN
Spain
and Portugal

Fine cuisine may not come to mind when you think of Spain or Portugal the way it does when you think of France, and you might not pick Spain or Portugal as a destination for food, the way you might pick Italy. But you ought to.

Spanish food is often confused with the cuisine of Mexico and Latin America, which is somewhat understandable given Spain's colonial past, but Spanish food is nothing like the food of the New World. While you will certainly find a *tortilla* on a menu, it will be an omelet, not the filled corn or flour wrapper we are accustomed to here in America. And you won't find refried beans or the traditional spicy hot peppers of Mexican cooking. Instead, you'll be treated to diverse regional specialties including *paella*, *gazpacho* and *sangria*, great cheeses, cured meats, as well as sausages and appetizers, called *tapas*, unlike anything else in the world.

The rich and full-flavored cuisine of **Portugal** has been greatly influenced by the country's explorer past. The Portuguese were the preeminent explorers of the 15th and 16th centuries, and brought back fruits, nuts, and spices that they incorporated into their dishes. Ingredients such as cinnamon, *piri piri* (chili peppers), nutmeg, cloves, and cashews are just a few of these.

Like Spain, Portuguese dishes vary from region to region. You'll find fresh fish and shellfish dishes throughout the country. Specialties include the national dish *bacalhau* (dried, salted cod), *leitão* (suckling pig) is popular in the northern part of the country, and *cozido à portuguesa* (stew of boiled sausages, potatoes, vegetables and meats) is another popular national dish. Nuns have created some of Portugal's delicious desserts such as *papo de anjo* ("angel's double chin"). It's made from whipped egg yolks, baked, and then boiled in sugar syrup. And don't forget to try Portuguese wine, especially *vinho verde* ("green wine" made from unripened grapes). It's young and slightly sparking. Port wine (*vinho do Porto*) is a fortified wine produced in the northern provinces of the country. It's typically a sweet, red wine, and comes in dry, semi-dry, and white varieties. You can't leave Portugal without sampling this dessert wine.

Even people who speak passable Spanish or Portuguese can have trouble reading a menu. Although you may know that the word for fish in Spanish is *pescado*, you might be surprised to discover *kokotxas* (fish glands, a Basque specialty) on a menu. If you think of it in terms of English, can you imagine a foreign traveler who speaks basic English and knows the word for meat, understanding what prime rib is? Or a porterhouse? Veggie platter, anyone? Buffalo wings? Sloppy joes?

Traveling requires a good guide. The same is true of dining. This guide can make the difference between a memorable evening and a nightmare or even just a dull one, but who wants a dull evening when you're on vacation? There is nothing worse than hiking all over a city looking for a good place to eat dinner, finding nothing, in near panic settling for whatever comes along next, having a lousy meal, then, upon leaving, discovering what looks like the best restaurant in the world right around the corner. Believe me, it happens all the time. The restaurant-guide portion of this book is a list of some of our favorite places in Spain and Portugal, and the menu-translator section will help you find your way around a menu written in Spanish or Portuguese. It gives you the freedom to enter places you might never have entered before and order dinner without shouting, pointing, or hand waving.

We know the panic of opening a menu without recognizing one word on it and the disappointment of being served something other than what you thought you'd ordered. This guide was created for travelers who want to enjoy, appreciate and experience authentic cuisine *and* know what they are eating.

Spain

Unpretentious and based on fresh ingredients, Spanish cuisine varies by region. Certain ingredients such as tomatoes, garlic, olive oil and sweet peppers can be found in dishes throughout Spain. Spanish cuisine hardly ever includes cream or butter. Complex sauces are rarely found in dishes except in the Basque country, the likely result of this region's proximity to France.

Spain has much to offer the traveler. If you want in-depth coverage of Spain's many and varied travel destinations, check out Open Road's *Best of Spain*. What follows are places of interest and dining specialties for all regions of Spain.

*Central Spain: Madrid, Castilla-La Mancha
and Castilla y León*

Spain's capital is located on a plateau in the center of the country. Madrid is truly one of Europe's great cities and to try to list Madrid's

attractions would require another guide. Although travelers come to visit Madrid's monuments, medieval central city and museums such as the Prado, they soon get caught up in the lively nightlife that makes Madrid unique. The nightly *tapas* scene alone is worth a trip to Madrid.

The museum-like walled city of Toledo is only a day trip away from Madrid. But don't just come here for the day. Toledo, with its cobbled walkways, is a comfortable and easy-to-manage city that comes to life in the evening. Other towns worth a visit are the walled city of Ávila, Segovia (with its Roman aqueduct, churches and fortress), the historic university city of Salamanca, and Cuenca, located on a dramatic gorge, famous for its *casas colgadas* (hanging houses) and modern art museum. Toward the Portuguese border is the fortified hilltop town of Ciudad Rodrigo in Castilla y León.

In Madrid, you can find the cuisine of all of Spain's regions. Two truly Madrid dishes are *callos a la madrileña* (tripe stew with peppers, sausage, ham and tomatoes) and *cocido madrileño* (stew made from meat, vegetables and chickpeas). Roasted meats (*asados*) are found on the menus throughout central Spain. You'll find many dishes featuring *perdiz* (partridge), *cochinillo* (suckling pig) and *manchego* (a hard, salty, rich and nutty cheese). *Farinato* (a sausage made from pork, flour and lard, generally eaten with fried eggs) is a specialty in Castilla y León. For dessert, try *buñuelos* (cream-filled pastries) and *bizcochos borrachos* (spongecake soaked in liquor).

Northern Spain: Galicia, Asturias, Cantabria, Navarra, La Rioja and Aragon

Known for its beautiful coast, Galicia (in northwestern Spain) is often compared to England or Ireland because of its rainy winter weather and its Celtic heritage. You'll find bagpipes and signs in *gallego* (the local language which is a mix of Spanish and Portuguese). Santiago de Compostela is visited every July by Christian pilgrims who travel through northern Spain to the cathedral which is believed to contain the remains of St. James the Apostle. A trip to Pontevedra will allow you to experience a typical Galician small town.

Cantabria has a rocky coastline and spectacular mountains. The north-central Atlantic coastal regions of Asturias and Cantabria aren't as crowded as the southern coastal areas, but still feature beach resorts such as Santander. One town that is nicely preserved is Santillana del Mar. From the Austurian village of Panes, you can explore the scenic mountain area of Picos de Europa.

Bordering on France in the northeast of Spain, Navarra's architecture reflects its many former rulers (from Arabic to Celtic). Most come here to visit the capital Pamplona, an interesting city that should not just be known for its annual Fiesta de San Fermín. You know this festival for its famous "running of the bulls."

The small region of La Rioja is south of the Basque country and west of Navarra. This is a wine-producing region and most travelers come here for wine tasting. *Bodegas* (wine or sherry cellars) can be found in many of the small towns in this region. Here you can sample some of the best Spanish wines in some of the least touristy towns of Spain. Elciego, southwest of Pamplona, is home to a Frank Gehry-designed hotel complex and renowned restaurant (Echaurren). There's also a winery, wine bar, wine tastings, a wine museum, a vinotherapy spa where you can bathe in wine … (I guess that's why they call it the "City of Wine.")

On the border with France near the northeast corner of Spain, Aragón is visited by few travelers and loved by hunters, sportsmen and skiers. The capital is Zaragoza which has a small old district with landmarks from Arab, Roman, Gothic and Renaissance eras. This area, with its cool summer temperatures, can be quite a relief from the hot coastal areas. Aragón has the highest peaks of the Pyrenees (Pirineos) mountains that separate Spain from France.

Seafood dominates the cuisine of Galicia, especially *pulpo* (octopus), *vieiras* (scallops) and *percebes* (barnacles). We once watched a Japanese couple pantomime an octopus to a waiter here and we were able to explain that they wanted octopus for dinner. It remains one of our favorite dining experiences. Galicia is also known for *caldo gallego* (meat and vegetable soup). Asturia is known for its *fabada* (pork, bean, sausage and bacon stew) and for *queso de Cabrales* (a strong blue cheese). In Cantabria, you'll find salmon, trout and *raba* (breaded, fried squid) on many menus. The cuisine of Navarra and Aragón stresses vegetables, chicken and pepper sauces. *Truchas a la Navarra* (trout baked with red wine and herbs) is the signature dish of Navarra.

Basque Country

The País Vasco (Euskadi) region is located along the Atlantic coast on the northeastern border with France. The Basques are said to be the oldest ethnic group in Europe and they have a unique language to prove it. San Sebastián (also known as Donostia) is known not only for its sandy beaches, but for its fine eating establishments. Bilboa is the home of the famous Guggenheim museum with its curved steel walls, a building that redefined the city. There are also some charming fishing villages along the Atlantic coast, such as Lekeitio.

The Basque country is said to have the best regional cuisine in Spain. The Basques are so interested in food that they have cooking clubs known as *Sociedades Populares*. *Kokotxas* (tender glands near the throat of cod) and *txangurro* (seasoned crabmeat) are two of the many innovative Basque dishes. Sauces play an important role in Basque cuisine. For dessert, try *intxaursalsa* (walnut cream).

Western Spain: Extremadura

If you travel from Madrid to Lisbon, you will pass through this arid and hot region of Spain, located in the western part of the country on the border with Portugal. Worth a visit are the beautiful fortified city of Cáceres whose old town has been impeccably preserved; Trujillo, a maze of cobblestone streets and home of the explorer Pizarro who brought back gold from South America to build many of the monuments here; Guadalupe (home of the black-faced Virgin whose shrine attracts pilgrims); and the capital Mérida, home of significant Roman ruins.

Lamb, pork and game dishes are popular in Extremadura. Spain's best-known ham (*jamón serrano*) comes from here. *Las migas* are pieces of bread soaked in water and then fried with dry peppers and pieces of bacon. Other regional specialties include *frite* (lamb fried with paprika) and *licor de bellota* (a liquor made from acorns).

Southern Spain: Andalusia and the Costa del Sol

Southern Spain is known as Andalusia. The Moors invaded this region from what is now Morocco. Andalusia retains the greatest Moorish influence in all of Spain. Many come here to visit lively Sevilla (we know it as Seville) with its winding streets, massive cathedral and Moorish palaces of the Alcazar. Spain's best-known *pueblo blanco* (traditional hilltop village of whitewashed buildings) is Ronda. If you have the time, you won't be disappointed with a side trip to these villages. Our favorite classic white town is Grazalema, filled with cobbled streets and buildings with iron balconies overflowing with flowers. Córdoba is home to the elaborate Mezquita, a red- and white-striped mosque. Granada, with its famous Moorish palace and gardens of Alhambra, is a jewel and

a must for travelers to this area. Forty-five minutes south of Granada, Salobreña is a whitewashed town clinging to a rock set back from the coastline surrounded by sugar-cane fields. Its very narrow streets and few tourists make it a great detour as you approach the touristy southern coast of Spain.

About halfway between Seville and the ancient port of Cádiz is the elegant town of Jerez de la Frontera. *Jerez* is the Spanish word for sherry. You'll find plazas lined with orange trees and streets filled with sherry *bodegas*.

East of Gibraltar is the famous Costa del Sol. There is something for everyone looking for sun and a party atmosphere. The wealthy visit Marbella, and the package-tour crowd hangs out in crowded, touristy and over-developed Torremolinos, Fuengirola and Benalmádena. Nerja, a resort town, manages to keep some of the fishing-village charm that is lacking in much of the region. Nerja is the location of the Balcón de Europa (Balcony of Europe), a lookout high above the sea.

In southern Andalusia, you'll find seafood (the Costa del Sol is known for its fried seafood dishes) and *gazpacho*. There are many variations of this cold soup. The most common is tomato-based. Three ingredients are found in all variations: bread, vinegar and oil. *Gazpacho andaluz* is a wonderful chilled purée of tomatoes, vinegar, onions, green peppers, garlic, cucumbers and bread crumbs. The word *gazpacho* derives from *caspa*, which means leftovers or crumbs. *A la andaluza* usually means a dish with red peppers, tomatoes and garlic, but not always. *Alcachofas a la andaluza* are artichokes with bacon and ham. For dessert, try *alfajores*, small round cakes with almonds said to have been introduced by the Moors.

Eastern Spain: Barcelona, Catalonia (Catalunya),
Costa Brava, Valencia, Costa Blanca and Murcia

If you ask the question "Do you prefer Madrid or Barcelona?" you'll get a different response from everyone you ask. Madrid is much younger than Barcelona. Barcelona is a city filled with well-preserved medieval buildings, modern architecture and the famous cathedral and other fabulous structures by Gaudí. A great European city, Barcelona is home to a famous Picasso museum, the wonder-

ful Gothic Quarter (Barri Gòtic) and La Rambla (where all of Barcelona seems to stroll each evening). Nearby are Montserrat, known for its mountaintop Benedictine monastery, and the area around Sant Sadurní d'Anoia known for its *cava* (sparkling) wines. In the far northeast corner of Spain is the interesting ancient town of Girona. Just north of Barcelona toward the French coast is the Costa Brava. This resort area is less crowded than the Costa del Sol. Platja de Aro and Lloret de Mar are two of the best-known beach resorts. The small villages of Begur and Pals are in a great contrast to the beach resorts.

To the south of Barcelona, around the town of Sitges, is the Costa Dorada, and if you travel along the coast south and west you'll reach Valencia and the Costa Blanca. Sun lovers come to the resort towns of Benidorm and La Manga (located in the Murcia region). If you don't care for crowds, avoid Spain's southern and eastern coasts in high season.

The food in Catalonia is similar to the cuisine of French Provence. Don't miss the fish stews such as *zarzuela*. Fish and meat dishes are often combined with fruit or nuts. *Romesco de pescado* is a fish dish sometimes flavored with almonds, hazelnuts and pine nuts.

Paella was invented in Valencia. There are said to be over 1500 variations of this popular national dish of saffron-flavored rice and various ingredients. Saffron is the costliest spice in the world since it must be harvested by hand. Spain produces more saffron than any other country.

Balearic Islands

The Balearic islands are located in the Mediterranean Sea. These mountainous and subtropical islands have become popular with travelers from northern Europe and the United Kingdom, especially in the summer months. Each island has a different landscape and attitude. The capital, Palma de Majorca, is 130 miles from Barcelona. Majorca has a rocky coastline with many small coves and sandy beaches. If you are looking for tranquility, Minorca is your best bet. If you're looking for a party, try wild Ibiza. Formentera and Cabrera are solitary islands.

In addition to seafood, many dishes feature pork (called *porcella* here). *Sobrasada* (salami with paprika), *el tumbet* (a vegetable casserole featuring eggplant) and *oliaigua* (a water-based soup flavored with garlic, parsley and olive oil) are all specialties here. To cool yourself from all the sun, try *pellofa*, a drink of gin with ice, sugar and lemon.

Canary Islands

Off the coast of Africa, the Canary Islands are seven islands 620 miles south of Spain with an eternal spring climate. From volcanic semi-desert to sub-tropical to snow-capped Mt. Teide, these islands offer great diversity for the traveler. The islands are a huge tourist destination not only for Spaniards, but for other European visitors as well.

Some specialties of the Canary Islands are *pollo al canario* (lemon and chicken), *puchero canario* (meat and chickpea casserole), *rancho canario* (a stew of sausage, bacon, beans, potatoes and pasta) and *potaje canario* (a soup with vegetables, potatoes and garbanzo beans). For dessert, you'll likely find tropical fruit drenched in syrup.

Types of Eating Establishments in Spain

Asador: grill room, rotisserie.
Bodega: In the country, particularly in the vicinity of Jerez, a wine or sherry cellar. Generally, you may tour the facilities and purchase wine and sherry. Today they can be found in cities, too, but they are usually just stores and wine bars.
Cafetería: self-service cafeteria.
Cervecería: bar.

Comedor: dining room. You get a basic, inexpensive meal here. These eating establishments have become harder to find.

Fonda: inn (frequently serving food).

Hostería: informal restaurant, usually associated with an inn.

Marisquería: seafood restaurant that frequently has tanks of live seafood.

Merendero: an open-air snack bar.

Mesón: simple, local restaurant.

Parador: Since the late 1920s, Spain has converted castles, monasteries and palaces into nearly 90 *paradores*, beautiful and comfortable hotels located throughout the country. Although sometimes pricey, each *parador* has its own restaurant serving regional specialties. You can't go wrong dining at a *parador*.

Pastelería: pastry shop.

Restaurante: We think you can figure this out.

Salon de té: tea room.

Sidrería: cider house located in the Basque country offering cod dishes, steaks, cheese and, of course, cider.

Taberna: tavern.

Tasca: bar serving small snacks (*tapas*) or larger portions (*raciones*) with your drink. Tradionally, *tapas* bars served a *tapa* with your drink order, but today, there may be an additional charge for the *tapa*.

Tetería: tea shop.

Venta: country inn serving food.

Xampanyerie: bar found in and around Barcelona serving *cava* (sparkling wine).

Types of Eating Establishments in Portugal

Adega tipica: small eatery serving local dishes.

Casa de fados: restaurant featuring *fados* (melancholy folk songs).

Casa de pasto: inexpensive and informal eatery.

Cervejaria: tavern or beer garden.

Churrasqueira: family-style restaurant specializing in grilled food and barbeque.

Estalagem: inn, usually serving regional dishes.

Marisqueira: seafood restaurant.

How to Use This Guide

Like most restaurants throughout Europe, the menu is almost always posted outside of the establishment or in a window. This makes choosing a restaurant easy and fun as you "window shop" for your next meal. You can refer to our guide outside so you seem more informed inside!

Remember that the dish that you ordered may not be exactly as described in this guide. Every chef is (and should be) innovative. What we have listed for you in this guide is the most common version of a dish. And remember, if a menu has an English translation it does not mean that their translation is correct.

The menu-translator section of this guide includes not only the specialties of the regions of Portugal and Spain, but also wonderful dishes of other travel destinations such as Mexico, Central and South America, Puerto Rico, Cuba and the Dominican Republic.

Tipping
Restaurants automatically include a tax and service charge. It is still customary to leave a small tip unless the service or the food has been unsatisfactory. If the meal and service have been great, you may tip *up to* 10%. If you want to be safe, ask if the tip is included: *¿Esta incluida la propina?* (Spain), *Serviço incluido?* (Portugal).

IVA, the government tax on your bill, is not a charge for service.

If service is not included in your bill, you may want to leave the tip in cash. A tip added to your credit card bill does not always end up in the pocket of the server.

Meals and Mealtimes
Food is an important part of a Spaniard's day. Breakfast is usually no more than a cup of coffee and rolls. Some might, especially in Madrid, have *churros y porras*. *Churros* are loops and *porras* are sticks of deep-fried batter dipped in a cup of hot chocolate. The mid-day meal is usually served between 1 p.m. and 4 p.m. and is often the

most important meal of the day. Hors d'oeuvres (*entremeses*) and/or soup are followed by an egg or fish plate which is followed by a main dish, usually meat. Dessert is followed by coffee. Wine, and frequently lots of it, is served with this large midday meal. In the early evening, Spaniards begin to head for bars where they drink wine and sample assorted *tapas* before having a late dinner.

The Moors and Arabs left a great influence on the cuisine of Spain. Nowhere is that influence stronger than in Spanish desserts. The Moors introduced honey and almonds. Ground almonds frequently replace flour in baking, and egg whites are used as the leavening agent in cakes. Many desserts are flavored with lemon and orange zest. *Flan* (caramel custard) is the national dessert of Spain and enjoyed in all Latin American countries. It's custard made with eggs, milk, sugar and spices, poured into a mold and cooked in a double boiler. *Flan* is usually topped with caramel, but there are many other variations of this dessert. Chocolate, coffee and honey are just a few of the ingredients used in variations of *flan*. Not all flans are desserts, however. *Flan* can also be served as an appetizer made with cheese, salmon or asparagus.

It cannot be stressed enough that Spaniards eat extremely late. The evening meal is served between 10 p.m. and midnight. While some restaurants have begun to open earlier, especially in restaurants that are frequented by tourists, most Spaniards like to eat late, and you'll find a more genuine Spanish dining experience if you do, too. The Portuguese serve lunch from noon to 2 p.m. and dinner from around 7:30 p.m. to 10:00 p.m.

Tapas

The Spaniards love *tapas*. They are small amounts of nearly any kind of food, usually served with a small glass of wine. The time between lunch and dinner is usually when most Spaniards frequent *tapas* bars. You can have a *porción* (small sample) or a *ración* (a larger quantity). *Tapas* bars are open all day. The word *tapa* means lid or cover and comes from the practice of covering the jugs of wine with pieces of food on toast or plates. *Tapeo* is the act of bar hopping in the early evening, eating *tapas* and drinking, before Spain's late dinner hour. *Tascas* are bars that serve wine and *tapas*.

Many *tapas* bars do not take credit cards. It is usually cheaper to order at the bar rather than at a table in *tapas* bars.

Smoking
Smoking is banned in all bars and restaurants in Spain and Portugal.

Drinking in Spain and Portugal
Spanish wines are gaining popularity. The town of Valdepeñas produces the most table wines. Rioja is the most popular of the more expensive wines. *Reserva* or *Gran Reserva* on a wine bottle means that the wine is a better wine. The Spaniards love sherry (or *jerez*, as it is called in Spain) and there are several good national and local beers (*cervezas*). Throughout Spain, you'll find many varieties of *sangria*, a wine-and-fruit punch. The menu-translator portion of this guide also includes beverages, both alcoholic and non-alcoholic. In Portugal, you'll find *vinho verde* ("green wine" made from unripened grapes). It's young and slightly sparking. Port wine (*vinho do Porto*) is a fortified wine produced in the northern provinces of the country. It's typically a sweet, red wine, and comes in dry, semi-dry, and white varieties. You can't leave Portugal without sampling this dessert wine.

Water
Europeans joke that you can tell a U.S. tourist from his fanny pack, clothes and ubiquitous bottle of mineral water. Tap water is safe in all parts of Spain and Portugal, but mineral water is often served with meals.

Restaurants in this Guide
Each of our recommended restaurants offers something different. Some have great food and little ambiance. Others have great ambiance and adequate food. Still others have both. Our goal is to find restaurants that are moderately priced and enjoyable. All restaurants have been tried and tested. Not enough can be said for a friendly welcome and great service. No matter how fabulous the meal, the experience will always be better when the staff treats you as if they actually want you there rather than simply tolerating your presence.

Times can change and restaurants can close, so do a walk-by earlier in the day or the day before, if possible. Our full list of restaurants starts on page 117.

Tips for Budget Dining

There is no need to spend a lot of money in Spain and Portugal to have good food. There are all kinds of fabulous foods to be had inexpensively all over the country.

Eat at a neighborhood restaurant or *tapas* bar. You'll usually know the price of a meal before entering, as almost all restaurants post the menu and prices in the window. Never order anything whose price is not known in advance unless you're feeling adventurous.
Delis and food stores can provide cheap and wonderful meals.
Buy some cheese, bread, wine and other snacks and have a picnic. Remember to pack a corkscrew and eating utensils when you leave home.

The Spanish eat very late. Sometimes when you go to a *tapas* bar (or several) before dinner, you find that you really aren't up to a late-night dinner.

Lunch, even at the most expensive restaurants listed in this guide, always has a lower price. So, have lunch as your main meal.
Restaurants that have menus written in English (especially those near tourist attractions) are almost always more expensive than neighborhood restaurants.

If you're concerned about the cost of a meal, the menu of the day *menú del día* (Spain), *prato do dia* (Portugal) is usually a better value for your money than purchasing food *á la carte*.

Street vendors generally sell inexpensive and good food. For the cost of a cup of coffee or a drink, you can linger at a café and watch the world pass you by for as long as you want. It's one of Europe's greatest bargains.

And don't eat at McDonald's, for God's sake.

Portuguese Pronunciation Guide

If you are looking for a comprehensive guide to speaking Portuguese, this is not the the right place. What follows is simply a few tips for speaking Portuguese and a very brief pronunciation guide. Don't try to speak Spanish in Portugal. French is the linguistic cousin to Portuguese. Words are stressed on the last syllable, but generally if a word ends with a, e or o, the stress falls on the next to the last syllable.

a like a in father or a in bang

â like ung in hung

ã a nasal "ung"

b as in English

c usually like c in cat, but followed by e or i like c in city

ç like s in sun

ch like sh in shun

d as in English

e usually like e in bet (when stressed). Sometimes like a in gate. When not stressed, like er in mother. At the beginning of a word, like i in bit

é like e in bet

ê like a in gate

f as in English

g usually like g in good, but when followed by e or i like s in measure

h is silent

i like ee in weed

j like s in pleasure

k as in English

l as in English

lh like li in million

m like m in met. Between a vowel and a consonant or at the end of a word, it nasalizes the vowel

n as in English

nh like ny in canyon

o like o in note, oo in soon or aw in raw

ô like o in note

p as in English

q like k in kite when qui or que. Like the qu in quick when qua or quo

qü like qu in quick

r similar to h at the beginning of a word. Single tap on the roof of the mouth when in the middle of a word

rr similar to h

s like s in sit. At the end of a word, like sh. Between two vowels or before b, d, g, l, m, n, r or v, like z in zebra

ss like s in sun

t as in English

u like oo in moon

v as in English

w as in English

x has four pronunciations: ks as in explicar, sh as in xarope, z as in examinar and s as in execto

z as in English

English to Portuguese

This is a brief listing of some familiar English food and food-related words that you may need in a restaurant setting. It is followed by a list of phrases that may come in handy.

allergy, alérgico

anchovy, anchova

another, outro

appetizer, entrada

apple, maçã

artichoke, alcachofra

ashtray, cinzeiro

asparagus, espargos

bacon, toucinho

baked, (no) forno

banana, banana

bathroom, banho

bean, feijão

beef, bife

beef steak, bife

beer, cerveja

beverages, bebida

big, grande

bill, conta

boiled, cozido

bottle, garrafa

bowl, tigela

braised, flamejado

bread, pão

breaded, empanado

bread roll, pãozinho

breakfast, pequeno-almoço

broccoli, brócolos

broth, canja/caldo

burnt, queimado

butter, manteiga

cabbage, couve

cake, bolo

calories, calorias

candle, vela

carbonated, com gás

carrot, cenoura

cash (money), dinheiro

cashier, caixa

cereal, cereal

chair, cadeira

change (coins), troca

cheap, barato

check (bill), conta

cheers, saúde

cheese, queijo

cherry, cereja

chicken, frango

chocolate, chocolate

cigarette, cigarro

clams, amêijoas

closed, fechado

cod, bacalhau

coffee, café

coffee with milk, café com leite

cold, frio

corkscrew, saca-rolhas

corn, milho

cost (price), preço

cream, creme

cucumber, pepino
cutlery, talheres
cutlet, costeleta
cup, chávena
decaffeinated, descafeinado
dessert, sobremesa
diabetic, diabético
diet, alimentação/dieta
dinner (supper), jantar
dirty, sujo
dish (plate), prato
drink, bebida
dry, seco
duck, pato
egg, ovo
eggplant, berinjela
enough, suficiente
expensive, caro
fast, rápido
fish, peixe
food, comida
food poisoning, envenanamento alimentar
fork, garfo
free, grátis
french fries, batatas fritas
fresh, fresco
fried, frito
fruit, fruta
game (meat), caça
garlic, alho
gin, gin
glass, copo
goat (baby), cabrito
goose, ganso
grape, uva

grapefruit, toranja
greasy, gorduroso
green bean, feijão-verde
grilled, grelhado
half (portion), meia dose
ham, presunto (smoked)/fiambre (cured)
hamburger, hamburger
hangover, ressaca
honey, mel
hors-d'oeuvre, entrada
hot, quente
ice, gelo
ice cream, sorvete/gelado
included, incluído
juice, sumo
ketchup, ketchup
knife, faca
kosher, kosher
lamb, borrego/carneiro
large, grande
lemon, limão
less, menos
lettuce, alface
little (small), pequeno
liver, fígado
lobster, lagosta
lunch, almoço
match, fósforo
mayonnaise, maionese
meat, carne
medium (cooked), médio
melon, melão
menu, ementa
milk, leite
mineral water, água mineral

mineral water (sparkling), água com gás

mixed, mista

more, mais

mushroom, cogumelo

mussel, mexilhão

mustard, mostarda

napkin, guardanapo

no, não

non-alcoholic, sem alcool

non-smoker, não-fumador

nut, noz

olive oil, azeite de azeitona

olive, azeitona

omelette, omeleta

onion, cebola

only, sozinho

orange, laranja

orange juice, sumo de laranja

order, to, pedir

organic, orgânico

oyster, ostra

pastry, pastelaria

peach, pêssego

peanut, amendoim

pear, pêra

peas, ervilhas

pepper (spice), pimenta

pepper (vegetable), pimento

pineapple, ananás

plate (dish), prato

please, por favor

plum, ameixa

pork, porco

potato, batata

poultry, aves

rabbit, coelho

rare, mal passado

raspberry, framboesa

raw, crú

receipt, recibo/factura

reservation, reserva

restroom, casa de banho

rice, arroz

roast, assado

roll, papo seco/pães

salad, salada

salad dressing, molho

salmon, salmão

salt, sal

sandwich, sanduíche/sandes

sauce, molho

sausage, salsicha

scrambled eggs, ovos mexidos

seafood, marisco

service, serviço

shellfish, mariscos

shrimp, camarão (camarões)

small, pequeno

smoked, defumado

smoke, fumo

snails, caracóis

sole, linguado

soup, sopa

sour, azedo

spaghetti, espaguete

sparkling, espumante

specialty, especialidade

spicy, picante

spinach, espinafre

spoon, colher

stale (bread), duro

steak, bife
steam, vapor
stew (fish), caldeirada
straw (drinking), palhinha
strawberry, morango
sugar, açúcar
sugar substitute, sacarina
sweet, doce
table, mesa
tea, chá
tea with lemon, chá com limão
tea with milk, chá com leite
temperature, temperatura
thank you, obrigado (masculine)
  obrigada (spoken by a woman)
tip, gorjeta
toasted, torrado
tomato, tomate
toothpick, palito
translate, traduza
trout, truta
tuna, atum
turkey, perú
undercooked (rare), mal passado
veal, vitela
vegetables, legumes
vegetarian, vegetariano (a)
vinegar, vinagre
waiter, empregado
waitress, empregada
water, água
watermelon, melancia
well done, bem passado
wine, vinho
wine list, lista de vinhos
wine (red), vinho tinto

wine (rosé), vinho rosé
wine (sparkling), vinho
  espumante
wine (white), vinho branco
with, com
without, sem
yes, sim
yogurt, yogurte
zucchini, courgette

Helpful Phrases

please, por favor *(poor-fah-vor)*
thank you, obrigado
  (oh-bree-gah-doo)
good morning, bom dia
  (bohn *dee*-ah)
good afternoon, boa tarde
  (boh-ah tar-deh)
good evening/night, boa noite
  (boh-ay noy-teh)
goodbye, adeus *(ah-deh-oosh)*
I am sorry., Desculpe.
  (dish-kool-peh)
Do you speak English?, Fala
  inglês? *(fah-lah een-glaysh)*
I don't speak Portuguese., Não
  falo português.
  (now fah-loo poor-too-gaysh)
excuse me, com licença
  (kohn li-*sehn*-sah)
I don't understand., Não
  com preendo.
  (now kohn-pree-ayn-doo)
I'd like, Gostaria
  (goosh-tah-ree-ah)
...to reserve, de reservar
  (de reh-zehr-var)

25

a table for, uma mesa para
  *(oo-mah **may**-zah **par**-rah)*
one uma *(oo-mah),* **two** dois
  (doysh), **three** três *(traysh),* **four**
  quatro *(**kwah**-troo),* **five** cinco
  *(**seeng**-koo),* **six** seis *(saysh),*
seven sete *(**seh**-teh),* **eight** oito
  *(**oy**-too),* **nine** nove *(**nah**-veh),* **ten**
  dez *(dehsh)*
now, agora *(ah-**goh**-rah)*
today, hoje *(**oh**-zheh)*
tomorrow, amanhã *(ah-ming-**yah**)*
by the window, perto da janela
  *(**pehr**-too dah zhah-**neh**-tah)*
inside/outside, dentro/fora
  *(**dehn**-troo/**foh**-rah)*
with a view, com vela vista
  *(kohn **oo**-mah **veesh**-tah)*
where is...?, Onde é...?
  *(**ohn**-deh eh)*
the toilet, casa de banho
  *(**kah**-zah deh **bahn**-yoo)*
the bill, conta *(**kohn**-tah)*
a mistake (error), erro
service included, serviço incluída
  *(sehr-**vee**-soo een-kloo-**ee**-doo)*
Credit cards?, Cartão de crédito?
  *(kar-**tow** deh **kreh**-dee-too)*
How much?, Quanto custa?
  *(**kwahn**-too **koosh**-tah)*
I did not order this., Não pedi isto.
  *(now-peh-**dee** **eesh**-too)*
this is , este é *(**eesh**-too eh)*
cold, frio *(**free**-oo)*
undercooked, malcozinhado
  *(mahl-koo-zeen-**yah**-doo)*

26

overcooked, queimado
  *(kay-**mah**-doo)*
delicious, delicioso
  *(deh-lee-see-**oh**-zoo)*
cheap/expensive, barato/caro
  *(bah-**rah**-too/**kah**-roo)*
good/bad, bom/mau *(bohn/mow)*
less/more, menos/mais
  (may-noosh/mish)
I am a..., Sou *(soh)*
vegetarian, vegetariano
  *(veh-zheh-tar-ree-**ah**-noo)*
allergic, alérgico
  *(ah-**lehr**-zhee-koo)*
diabetic, diabético
  *(dee-ah-**beh**-tee-koo)*
drunk, bêbado *(**bay**-bah-doo)*
I cannot eat..., Não posso
  comer... *(now **pos**-soo koh-mehr)*
meat, carne *(**kar**-neh)*
pork, porco *(**por**-koo)*
shellfish, mariscos *(mah-**reesh**-koosh)*
closed, fechado *(feh-**shah**-too)*
open, aberto *(ah-**behr**-too)*
monday, segunda-feira
  *(seh-goon-dah **fay**-rah)*
tuesday, terça-feira
  *(tehr-sah **fay**-rah)*
wednesday, quarta-feira
  *(kwar-tah **fay**-rah)*
thursday, quinta-feira
  *(**keen**-tah **fay**-rah)*
friday, sexta-feira
  *(saysh-tah **fay**-rah)*
saturday, sábado *(**sah**-bah-doo)*
sunday, domingo *(doo-**meeng**-goo)*

Portuguese to English

à/à moda de, in the style of
abacate, avocado
abacaxi, pineapple
abóbora, pumpkin
abobrinha, zucchini
açafrão, saffron
acará/acarajé, fritters made from black beans and fried dried shrimp
acelga, Swiss chard
acepipes, hors d'ouevres/appetizers
acompanhamento, side dish/vegetables
açorda, a thick soup. Bread is the main ingredient and there are
   many versions
açorda alentejana, *açorda* with garlic, poached eggs, coriander,
   olive oil
açorda de bacalhau, *açorda* with dried cod
açorda à moda Sesimbra, *açorda* with garlic, fish and coriander
açúcar, sugar
agri-doce, sweet and sour sauce
agrião, watercress
água, water. *Água de torneira* is tap water
água gelada, ice water
água mineral, mineral water
água com gas, mineral water with carbonation
água sem gas, mineral water without carbonation
aguardente, brandy/aquavitae
aipo, celery
alcachofra, artichoke
alcaparra, caper
alcoólico, alcoholic
alecrim, rosemary
alentejana, usually means with tomatoes and onions
aletria, thin noodles (vermicelli). This also can refer to a dessert
   made with vermicelli, eggs and cream
alface, lettuce
alheira, garlic sausage
alheira à transmontana, garlic sausage served with fried potatoes,
   fried eggs and cabbage
alho, garlic
alhoporro, leek
à lista, a la carte
almoço, lunch
almôndega, fish or meat ball
amanteigado, buttered

amargo, bitter/sour

amêijoa, small clam

amêijoas à Bulhão Pato, clams fried in olive oil with coriander and garlic. This dish is named after a Portuguese poet

amêijoas à espanhola, baked clams with onions, garlic, tomatoes, peppers and herbs

amêijoas ao natural, clams steamed with herbs (and served with lemon juice and melted butter)

ameixa, plum

ameixa seca, prune

amêndoa, almond

amendoim, peanut

à moda de, in the style of

amora, blackberry

amor em pedaços, bars made with cookie dough and topped with almonds and merengue (means "love in pieces")

ananás, pineapple

anchova, anchovy

anho à moda do Minho, roast lamb and rice dish

aniz, anis

angu, cassava root or corn boiled in water and salt

ao, in the style of

ao natural, plain. Also refers to drinks served at room temperature

ao ponto, medium

aperitivo, aperitif

arenque, herring

arroz, rice

arroz árabe, fried rice with dried fruits and nuts

arroz à valenciana, rice with pork, chicken and seafood

arroz brasileiro/arroz simples, rice sautéed in garlic, onion and oil before boiling

arroz com feijão, rice browned in onion, oil and garlic before boiling, and served with black beans on the side

arroz de Cabidela, risotto with giblets and chicken blood

arroz de frango, baked chicken and rice

arroz de manteiga, rice cooked in water and butter

arroz de marisco, rice with seafood

arroz de pato no forno, duck cooked in rice with bacon and pork sausage

arroz doce, sweet rice pudding

arroz do povo, rice cooked with slices of meat, onion beans and garlic

arroz mineiro, rice cooked with carrots, potatoes and minced meat

arroz tropeiro, rice with salted and dried meat

aspargo, asparagus

aspide, aspic

assado, roast/roasted

assado nas brassas, broiled
atum, tuna
aveia, oats
avelã, hazelnut
aves, poultry
avezia, flounder
azeda, sorrel
azedo, sour
azeite, olive oil
azeitona, olive
azeitona preta, black olive
azeitona recheada, stuffed olive
azeitona verde, green olive
azeitona verde de Elvas, green olive

ORDERING MEAT

well done – *bem passado*

medium – *médio/no ponto*

rare – *mal passado*

raw – *crú*

---

bacalhau, cod. Usually dried and salted. It's said that the Portuguese
  have as many ways to prepare cod as there are days in the year.
bacalhau à Brás, cod fried with onions and potatoes topped with
  beaten eggs then baked
bacalhau à Gomes de Sá, cod fried with onions, garlic, boiled
  potatoes (and usually served with hard-boiled eggs)
bacalhau à portuguesa, cod between layers of potatoes and
  tomatoes and baked
bacalhau à provinciana, cod, potato and turnips au gratin
bacalhau à transmontana, cod braised with cured pork, garlic,
  parsley, tomatoes and wine
bacalhau à Zé do Pipo, cod with an egg sauce
bacalhau com natas no forno, boiled cod baked with potatoes
  and cream
bacalhau de caldeirada, cod braised with tomatoes, onions, garlic,
  coriander and parsley
bacalhau cozido, boiled cod with green beans and carrots
bacalhau cozido com todos, poached cod served with boiled
  cabbage, potatoes and eggs
bacalhau fresco à Portuguesa, fresh cod with rice and vegetables
bacalhau na brasa, barbecued dried cod
bacon, bacon
bagas, berries
batata, potato. *Batata assada* **is a** baked potato
batata doce, sweet potato
batata frita, French Fry
batata sotê, boiled parsley potatoes
baunilha, vanilla
bavaroise, egg white and cream dessert
bebida, drink/beverage
bem casados, sugar cookies bound together with a filling
  (means "well married")
bem passado, well-done
berbigão, a kind of cockle

berinjela, eggplant
besugo, sea bream
betteraba, beet
bica, espresso
bifana, a slice of pork tenderloin in a bread roll
bife, steak
bife a cavalo, beef topped with a fried egg
bife à cortador, beef fried in garlic-butter
bife à milanesa, breaded veal scallops
bife à portuguesa, steak with a mustard sauce and usually topped
   with a fried egg
bife de atum, tuna steak
bife de cebolada, steak with onions
bife de espadarte, swordfish steak fried with potatoes and onions
bife de javali, wild boar steak
bife de vaca, steak
bife de vaca com ovo a cavalo, steak with an egg on top
bife grelhado, grilled steak
bifinhos de porco, small slices of pork
bifinhos de vitela, veal served with Madeira wine
bifinhos na brasa, slices of barbecued beef
biscoito, cookie
boi, beef
bola, scoop
bola de Berlim, donut (usually jelly-filled)
bolacha, cookie
bolaichas, crackers
bolinho de bacalhau, deep-fried cod ball
bolinho de queijo, deep-fried cheese ball
bolo, cake
bolo caseiro, home-made cake
bolo de carne, deep-fried ball of dough with a meat center/filling
bolo de chocolate, chocolate cake
bolo de nozes, walnut cake
bolo inglês, spongecake containing dried fruit
bolo podre, honey- and cinnamon-flavored cake
bolo rei, a Christmas ring cake
bomba de creme, cream puff
bombom de uva, grape surrounded by a sugar and egg mixture
borracho, young pigeon
borrego, lamb
branco, white
brande, brandy
brasa, charcoal-grilled
brigadeiros, rich chocolate fudge-like dessert, usually in a ball shape
brioche, croissant
broa, dark bread with a hard crust from northern Portugal

brócolos, broccoli
bruto, extra-dry
cabeça, head. *Cabeça de pescada* is a fish head dish
cabidela, giblets
cabreiro, goat's cheese
cabrito, baby goat. *Cabrito assado* is roast baby goat
caça, game
cacau, cocoa
caçador(a), simmered in wine with onions, carrots and herbs
cachola frita, fried pig's heart dish
cachorro quente, hot dog
cachucho, small sea bream
café, coffee. *Café estilo Americano* is American-style coffee
café da manhã, breakfast
café com leite, coffee with milk
café duplo, two espressos in one cup
café glacé, iced coffee
café instantâneo, instant coffee
cafezinho, strong coffee with sugar
caju, cashew nut
calamar, squid
caldeirada, fish stew with tomatoes, onions, potatoes, wine and herbs
caldeirada à fragateira, fish and mussels in tomato and herbs
caldeirada à moda da Póvoa, sea bass, eel, cod and hake, simmered
    with tomatoes and olive oil
caldeirada de enguias, eel *caldeirada*
caldo, soup/broth
caldo de aves, poultry (usually chicken) soup
caldo verde, thick soup with cabbage, potatoes and pork sausage
camarão (camarões), shrimp
camarão-carne, fried pastry filled with meat
camarão-peixe, fried pastry filled with fish
camarão frito, fried shrimp
camarão seco, dried shrimp
camarões empanados, shrimp fried in batter
camarões à Baiana, shrimp in a spicy tomato sauce
camarões à paulista, shrimp marinated in garlic, onion, lemon juice,
    vinegar and fried in oil
camarões grandes, jumbo shrimp
cambuquira, squash stewed with meat
canapé, small open-faced sandwich
canela, cinnamon
canja, rice and chicken stew
canja de galinha, chicken stew
capão, capon
caqui, persimmon
caracol (caracóis), snail. This also refers to a snail-shaped bun
    usually filled with currants

caranguejo, crab
carapau, similar to a sardine
carapau de escabeche, *carapau* fried and in a sauce of olive-oil,
    fried onions, garlic and vinegar
cardápio, menu
caril, curry
carmelizado, glazed
carne, meat
carne à jardineira, meat and vegetable stew
carne assado, roast meat
carne de carneiro, mutton
carne de porco, pork
carne de porco à alentejana, marinated pork fried with clams
carne de sol, meat which is salted and dried in the sun
carne de vaca, beef
carne de vinha, pickled pork dish
carne de vitela, veal
carneiro, lamb
carneiro guisado, lamb stewed with tomatoes, parsley,
    garlic and bay leaf
carne picada, minced meat
carne seca, dried meat
carnes frias, cold cuts
carta, flounder
carta de vinhos, wine list
caseiro, home-made
casquinhas de siri, crab meat served in a shell
casquinho de caranguejo, baked crab meat
casquinho de lagosta, lobster prepared with butter, onion, milk
    and potatoes and served in its shell
castanha, chestnut
castanha de caju, cashew
cataplana, steamed in a copper pan /shellfish and ham stew
catupiri, fresh fat cheese made from cow's milk
cavala, mackerel
ceia, dinner
cebola, onion. *Cebolada* **is** fried onion (a garnish)
cenoura, carrot
centeio, pão de, rye bread
cereja, cherry
cerveja, beer
cerveja branca, lager
cerveja de pressão, draft beer
cerveja preta, dark, bitter beer
cevada, barley.
chá, tea. *Chá gelado* is iced tea
chá com limão, tea with lemon

chá de ervas, herbal tea
chá de limão, hot lemon tea
champanhe, champagne
chanfana de porco, pork casserole
chantily, whipped cream
charlotte, cookies with cream and fruit
chávena, cup
cherne, a type of grouper
chicória, chicory/endive
chinès, Chinese
chispalhada, pig's feet-based stew
chispe, pig's foot
choco, cuttlefish

choco com tinta, cuttlefish cooked in its own ink
chocolate, chocolate
chocolate quente, hot chocolate
chopp, draft beer
chouriça/chouriço, spicy smoked pork sausage (with paprika)
chuchu, summer squash
churrasco, barbecued meats and sausages grilled on skewers
churrasco à Gaúcha, grilled meats
churros, thin long fritters
cidra, cider
cimbalino, small espresso
coco, coconut
codorniz, quail
coelho, rabbit
coelho à caçadora, rabbit with rice and potatoes
coelho assado, roast rabbit
coelho de escabeche, marinated rabbit
coentro, coriander
cogumelo, mushroom
colorau, paprika
colher, spoon
com, with
com gás, carbonated
com gelo, with ice
comida, meal
comida congelada, frozen food
cominha, caraway seed
compota, stewed fruit
congro, conger eel
conquilhas, baby clams
conta, check (the bill)
copo, glass
coquetel de camarão, shrimp cocktail
coração, heart

coracãoes de alcachofa, artichoke hearts
cordeiro, lamb
cortada, sliced
corvina, croaker fish
costeca, ribsteak
costeleta/costoleta, cutlet/chop
costeleta de porco, pork chop

IS THE TIP INCLUDED?

A gorjeta esta incluída?

costelinhas de carneiro, lamb chops
courgette, zucchini
couve, cabbage
couve à mineira, green cabbage and bacon
couve branca, white cabbage
couve-de-Bruxelas, Brussels sprouts
couve-flor, cauliflower
couve galega, galician cabbage (somewhat bitter)
couve lombarda, savoy cabbage
couve portuguesa, cabbage which is similar to *couve galega*
couvert, cover charge
couve roxa, red cabbage
coxinha, pastry filled with chicken, meat, shrimp or cheese
cozido, cooked/boiled/boiled stew. *Cozido ao vapor* means steamed
cozido à brasileira, stew with many ingredients including meats,
    sausages, plantains, sweet potatoes and corn on the cob
cozido à portuguesa, stew of boiled sausages, potatoes, vegetables
    (usually carrots, turnips and cabbage) and meats
cozido em lume brando, simmered
cozidos, ovos, hard-boiled eggs
creme, cream
creme de abacate, sweet avocado cream dessert
creme de cogumelos, cream of mushroom soup
creme de mariscos, cream of seafood soup
crepe, crepe
creme de leite, fresh cream
criação, livestock
cristalizada, candied
croquetes de camarões, shrimp croquettes
croissant, crescent roll
crú/crua, raw
crustáceo, crustacean
cubo de gelo, ice cube
damasco, apricot
descafeinado, decaffeinated
dióspiro, persimmon
diversos, assorted
dobrada/dobradinha, tripe
dobrada à moda do Porto, tripe and bean dish
doce, sweet

doce de laranja, marmalade
doce de ovos, egg custard
dourada, dory (a saltwater fish)
dourado, browned
e, and
éclair, éclair
ementa, menu. *Ementa do dia* is menu of the day
ementa fixa, fixed-priced menu
ementa turística, tourist menu (usually fixed-priced)
empada, small pie
empadinha, empanada (turnover filled with various ingredients)
empadão, large pie
empadão de batata, minced meat with mashed potato topping (shepherd's pie)
empanado, breaded
encharcada, dessert made of eggs and almonds
enchidos, assorted pork made into sausage
endívia, endive
enguia, eel
ensopado, stew
entradas, appetizers
entrecosto, sparerib
ervanço, chickpea
ervas, herbs
ervilha, pea
ervilhas reboçadas, buttered peas with bacon
escabeche, sauce of olive-oil, garlic, fried onions and vinegar
escalfado, poached
escalope, veal scallop (thin slices of veal)
escalope ao Madeira, veal scallop in Madeira wine
escalope de vitela, veal scallop (thin slices of veal)
escalope panado, breaded veal scallop
esfirra, pastry filled with spiced meat
espadarte, swordfish
espaguete, spaghetti
espaguete à bolognese, spaghetti in a tomato and meat sauce
espargo, asparagus
esparregado, creamy purée of assorted greens
especial da casa, specialty of the house
especiaria, spice
espetada, kebab
espeto, roasted on a spit
espinafre, spinach
espinafres gratinados, browned spinach with cheese sauce
espumante, sparkling
estragão, tarragon
estrelados, ovos, fried eggs

estufada, stew
estufado, braised/stewed
esturjão, sturgeon
expresso, espresso
faca, knife
faisão, pheasant
farinha, flour
farinha de aveia, oatmeal
farofa, cassava-root meal browned and buttered
farófias, meringues floating in a cream sauce ("floating island")
farturas, long, thin fritters
fatia, slice
fatias da China, baked egg yolks topped with syrup and cinnamon
    and served cold
fatias douradas, french toast
fatias recheadas, slices of bread with fried minced meat
favas, broad beans
febras de porco à alentejana, pieces of grilled pork fillet
feijão (feijões), bean
feijão à brasileira, meat and black bean dish
feijão branco, navy bean
feijão carrapato, green bean
feijão catarino, pink bean
feijão encarnado, red bean
feijão frade, black-eyed bean
feijão guisado, bean dish stewed with bacon in tomato sauce
feijão-manteiga, beans cooked and browned in butter and parsley
feijão preto, black bean
feijão tropeiro, black bean dish (fried with meat which has been
    salted and dried in the sun)
feijão verde, green bean
feijoada, black bean stew cooked with different meats and
    served with rice on the side
fiambre, ham
fígado, liver
fígado de aves, chicken liver
figo, fig
filé, steak, pork, chicken or veal slices fried and served
    with rice and beans
filé de peixe com molho de camarão, fish fillet with a shrimp sauce
filete, fillet
filhó, fritter
filhozes, sugar buns
fios de ovos, beaten egg yolk and sugar dessert
flamejado, braised
flan, caramel custard
fofos de bacalhau, codfish balls

folhado, puff pastry
folhado de carne, meat in pastry
folhado de salsicha, sausage roll
forma, pão de, white bread
forno, baked
framboesa, raspberry
frango, chicken
frango ao vinho, chicken breast in red wine sauce
frango assado, roast chicken
frango na púcara, chicken casserole flavored with port wine
frango no churrasco, barbecued chicken
frango no espeto, spit-roasted chicken
fresco, fresh
fressura de porco guisada, pork offal casserole
fricassé, casserole
frigideira, meat, seafood and/or vegetables topped with beaten eggs and baked. This is the word for frying pan
frio, cold
fritada de carne, meat and sausages fried with eggs and cheese
fritada de peixe, deep-fried fish
frito, fried/fritter
fruta, fruit
fruta em calda, fruit in syrup
fruta da época, seasonal fruit
fruta do conde, mixed tropical fruit
fruta cristalizada, candied fruit
fruta seco, date
fubá, cornflour
fumado, smoked
funcho, fennel
fundo de alcachofra, artichoke bottom
fungo, strong pungent mushroom
galantina, meat in gelatine
galão, large coffee with a lot of milk (served in a tall glass)
galeto na brasa, charcoal-broiled chicken
galinha, chicken
galinha corada, baked chicken
galinha de África, guinea fowl
galinhola, woodcock/snipe
gambas, shimp
ganso, goose
garfo, fork
garoupa, large grouper
garrafa, bottle
garrafeira, aged red wine
garoto, small coffee with milk
gasoso, carbonated

> **THE CHECK, PLEASE!**
>
> check – *conta*
> waiter – *empregado*
> waitress – *empregada*
> tip – *gorjeta*

gaspacho, purée of tomatoes, vinegar, onions, green peppers, garlic, cucumbers and bread crumbs (chilled)

gelado, ice cream

geléia, jelly/jam

gelo, ice

gengibre, ginger

ginja, a sour cherry

goiaba, guava

goiabada, guava paste

gordura, fat

gorjeta, tip

grão, chickpeas

grão-de-bico, chickpeas

grão com bacalhau, chickpea and dried cod stew

gratinado, oven browned

grelhado, grilled

grelos, turnip greens

groselha, red currant

guardanapo, napkin

guisado, stewed

hambúrguer, hamburger

hortaliça, green vegetable

hortelã, mint

imperial, a glass of beer (about 1/4 liter)

incluído, included

inhame, yam

iogurte, yoghurt

iscas, liver which is thinly sliced

iscas à portuguesa, thin slices of calf's liver marinated in garlic, wine and bay leaves (cooked in a shallow earthenware dish)

italiana, half of a strong espresso

jantar, dinner

jardineira, mixed vegetables

jarro, jug/carafe

javali, wild boar

lagosta, lobster

lagosta à americana, flaming lobster dish with Madeira wine, herbs, tomatoes and garlic

lagosta suada, lobster with tomatoes, garlic and onions in a port wine sauce

lagosta Thermidor, flaming lobster dish with white wine, herbs, spices and mustard

lagostins, crayfish

lagostim-do-rio, fresh-water crayfish

lampreia, lamprey fish

SPECIAL NEEDS	
allergic –	*alérgico*
diabetic –	*diabético*
diarrhea –	*diarréia*
diet –	*dieta*
dirty –	*sujo*
disabled –	
	deficiente físico
doctor –	*doutor*
drunk –	*bébado*
emergency –	*emergência*
food poisoning –	
envenanamento alimentar	
nausea –	*naúsea*
non-alcoholic –	*sem alcool*
non-smoker –	*não-fumador*

38

lampreia de ovos, dessert (in the shape of a lamprey fish) made of eggs and sugar

lanche, snack

laranja, orange

lasanha, lasagne

lavagante, lobster

lebre, hare

legumes, vegetables

legumes variados, mixed vegetables

leitão, suckling pig

leitão à Bairrada, roasted suckling pig (coated with a spicy sauce)

leitão assado, roast suckling pig

leitão recheado, roasted stuffed (with a spicy mixture) suckling pig

leite, milk

leite-creme, custard dessert

lentilha, lentil

leve, light (wine)

licor, liqueur

ligeira, a light snack (usually means a bite or two)

lima, lime

limão, lemon

limão verde, lime

limonada, lemon juice with sugar and water

língua, tongue

linguado, sole/flounder

linguado à meunière, sole (dipped in flour) sauteed in butter and served with lemon-juice and parsley

linguíça, pork sausage flavored with paprika

lista, list/menu

lista de preços, price list

lista dos vinhos, wine list

lombinho, pork loin

lombo, loin

lombo de vaca, sirloin

louro, bay leaf

lulas, squid

maçã, apple

maçã assada, baked apple

maçapão/massapão, marzipan/almond macaroon

macaxeira, cassava root

macedónia de frutas, fruit cocktail

Madeira, dry and sweet fortified wine

maduro, mature

maionese, mayonnaise. *Maionese de alho* is garlic mayonnaise

malaguete, hot pepper

mal passado, rare

Malvasia, a sweet Madeira wine

mamão, papaya
mandioca, cassava root
manga, mango
manjericão, basil
manteiga, butter. *Manteiga de amendoim* is peanut butter
manteiga queimada, a butter sauce used on fish dishes
mãozinhas de vitela guisadas, calves' feet dish
maracujá, passion fruit
maragarina/margarina, margarine
marinado, marinated
marinheira, a dish served with
  parsley, onions, wine and tomatoes
marisco, seafood
marmelada, quince jelly
marmelo, quince
massa, pastry/dough/pasta
mazagrin, iced coffee with lemon
medalhão, medallion
medalhão com arroz à piemontese, thick steak medallion wrapped
  in bacon and fried and served with rice with a creamy sauce
meia de leite, large white coffee
meia desfeita, dried cod fried with onions, vinegar and chickpeas and
  topped with garlic and hard-boiled eggs
meia dose, half portion
meia garrafa, half bottle
médio, medium
mel, honey
melancia, watermelon
melão, melon
melão com presunto, melon with cured ham
melão com vinho do Madeira, Madeira wine poured over melon
melão com vinho do Porto, port poured over melon
melo seco, semi-dry wine
merenda, snack
merengue, meringue
merengue de morango, strawberry meringue
mero, red grouper
meunière, à, sauteed in butter and served with lemon-juice
  and parsley
mexidos, ovos, scrambled eggs
mexilhão, mussel
mexerica, tangerine
migas, slices of bread dampened with olive oil and flavored
  with garlic
mil-folhas, napoleon
milho doce, sweet-corn
mingau, porridge

> **LET'S EAT!**
> breakfast – *pequeno almoço*
> lunch – *almoço*
> dinner – *jantar*

40

Minho, do, a dish served in a port wine, brandy, blood and
    spice sauce
mioleira, brains
miolos, brains
miolos mexidos com ovos, fried lamb brains and scrambled eggs
misto, mixed
miúdos de galinha, chicken giblets
mocotós, stewed calves' feet dish
moleza, soup made with pig's blood
molho, sauce/gravy
molho ao Madeira, Madeira wine sauce
molho apimentado, hot sauce
molho bearnaise, béarnise sauce (hollandaise sauce [melted butter,
    egg yolks and lemon juice] with vinegar, tarragon, shallots
    and wine
molho béchamel, white sauce (usually butter, milk [and/or cream]
    and flour)
molho branco, white sauce
molho de manteiga, butter and lemon sauce
molho à Espanhola, spicy garlic and onion sauce
molho holandês, sauce of melted butter, egg yolks and lemon juice
    (hollandaise sauce)
molho inglês, Worchestershire sauce
molho mornay, cheese sauce
molho tártaro, tartare sauce
molho veloutée, sauce made from egg yolks and cream
molho verde, green sauce of parsley, olive-oil, vinegar, spinach and
    coriander leaves
morango, strawberry
morango silvestre, wild strawberry
morcela, blood sausage
mortadela, bologna
moscatel, muscatel wine
mostarda, mustard
mousse, mousse
mousse de chocolate, chocolate mousse
muçuã, small turtle
muito mal passado, rare
mumu de siri, crabs cooked with tomatoes, onions and
    other ingredients
nabiça, turnip greens
nabo, turnip
não, no
não alcoôlico, non-alcoholic
napolitanas, cookies
nas brasas, braised
nata, cream

nata batida, whipped cream
natural, plain
nectarina, nectarine
nêspera, a small fruit similar to a plum
no churrasco, barbecued
no espeto, roasted on a spit
no forno, baked
no ponto, medium (meat)
noz, walnut
noz muscada, nutmeg
óleo, oil
óleo de amendoim, peanut oil
omeleta/omelete, omelette
omeleta simples, plain omelette
orelha, ear
osso, bone
ostras, oysters
ou, or
ouriço-do-mar, sea urchin
ovas, fish roe
ovo, egg
ovo cozido, boiled egg. *Ovo multo cozido* is a hard-boiled egg
ovo escalfado, poached egg
ovo estrelado, sunny side up egg
ovo estrelado com fiambre, fried ham and egg
ovos mexidos, scrambled eggs
ovos moles, beaten egg yolks in syrup
ovo nào multo cozido, soft-boiled egg
ovos queimados, sweet egg dish
ovos verdes, eggs stuffed with hard-boiled yolks which are mixed
  with an onion, vinegar and olive-oil mixture
pães, roll
paio, spicy cured pork
palha de ovos, egg pastries
palmito, palm shoots. They look like short white sticks and are eaten
  alone or in salads
panado, breaded
panqueca, pancake
pão, bread
pão branco, white bread
pão de centeio, rye bread
pão de forma, white bread
pão-de-ló, spongecake/angel food cake
pão de milho, corn bread
pão de queija, cheese bread
pão de trigo/pão integral, whole wheat bread
pão ralado, breadcrumbs

> **BE POLITE!**
>
> **please** – *por favor*
> **thank you** – *obrigado (spoken
> by a man)/obrigada (spoken by
> a woman)*
> **gentleman** – *senhor*
> **woman** – *senhora*
> **miss** – *menina*
> **I'm sorry.** – *Desculpe.*
> **Excuse me.** – *Com licença.*

pão torrado, toast
pãozinho, roll
papos de anjo, baked egg yolks topped with syrup (angel's chests)
papo seco, che
páprica, roll
para levar, "to go"
pargo, dentex (a fish)
parrilhada, grilled fish
passa, raisin
passa de uva, raisin
passado bem, well done
passado, mal, rare
pastéis, pastries
pastéis de bacalhau, dried cod fishcakes
pastéis de carne, puff pastry filled with meat
pastéis de queijo, cheese-filled fried dumpling
pasteis fritos, fried turnovers
pastel, small doughy snack (savory or sweet)
pastel de bacalhau, deep-fried dried cod and mash potato dish
pastel de Belém, custard pie
pastel de nata, custard pie
pastel folhado, flaky pastry
pastel de massa tenra, pie filled with minced meat
pastel de Santa Clara, small tart with almond filling
pastel de Tentúgal, pastry with a filling of beaten eggs
  cooked in syrup
pastelinhos de bacalhau, dried cod fish cakes
pasties de bacalhau, cod fish cakes
pataniscas, fritters
paté, pâté
pato, duck
pato ao tucupi, roast duck braised with carrots in cassava-root juice
pato com laranja, duck à l'orange
pé de moleque, peanut brittle
pé de porco, pig's feet
peito, breast. *Peito de frango* is a chicken breast
peixe, fish
peixe espada, sword fish
peixe frito, fried fish
peixinhos da horta, green bean fritters
pepino, cucumber. *Pepino de conserva* is a pickle
pequeno, small
pequeno almoço, breakfast
pêra, pear
pêra abacate, avocado
pêra bela helena, pear in a chocolate sauce
perca, perch

percebe, similar to a barnacle
perdiz, partridge
perdiz na púcara, partridge casserole
perna, leg
perna de carneiro assada, roast leg of lamb
perna de carneiro entremeada, stuffed roast leg of lamb
pernil, ham
perninhas de rã, frogs' legs
pêro, a type of apple
peru, turkey
peru assado à Califórnia, roast turkey with fruit
peru à brasileiro, stuffed and roasted turkey
pescada, whiting
pescada cozido dom todos, whiting served with green beans
  and potatoes
pescadinhas de rabo na boca, dish of fried whitings (served with
  their tails in their mouths)
pêssego, peach
pêssego careca, nectarine
petiscos, snacks (*tapas*)
pevide, seed. This can also refer to salted pumpkin seeds
picadinho, chopped meat mixed with tomatoes, onions and peppers
picado de carne, minced meat
picante, spicy/hot/highly seasoned
pimenta, pepper
pimentão, sweet pepper. *Pimentão picante* is a hot pepper, *pimentão
  verde* is a green pepper, and *pimentão vermelho* is a red pepper
piemontesa, creamy sauce made from grated cheese, butter,
  mushroom and wine. Usually served over rice
pingo, small coffee with milk
pinhão, pine nut
pinhoada, candied pine nut kernel
pio nonos, spongecake with guava paste
piperate, pepper stew
piri-piri, small hot peppers. This also refers to a seasoning made
  from hot peppers and olive oil
pistácio, pistachio
pitú, freshwater lobster
polvo, octopus
pombo, pigeon
ponche, punch
ponta de espargo, asparagus tip
porção, portion
porco, pork
porco recheado, roast stuffed pork
posta, slice of meat or fish
prato, dish/plate

prato do dia, plate of the day
prato especial da casa, specialty of the house
prato principal, main course
preço, price
preço variado, price varies. Abbreviated as p.v.
prego, small steak (usually in a bread roll)
prego no pão, steak sandwich
prego no prato, meat and fried egg roll
pré-pagamento, pay in advance
presunto, cured ham
pudim, pudding
pudim de bacalhau, dried cod loaf
pudim flan, caramel custard
pudim à portuguesa, custard flavored with brandy
puré, purée
puré de batata, mashed potatoes
queijinhos do céu, marzipan rolled in sugar
queijo, cheese
queijo cabreiro, goat cheese
queijo cardiga, goat and ewe's-milk cheese
queijo catupiri, cream cheese
queijo curado, white, mature, hard cheese
queijo da ilha, similar to cheddar and
   flavored with pepper. From the Azores
queijo da serra, a goat's cheese found in northeastern Portugal
queijo de cabra, goat's cheese
queijo de ovelha, sheep's cheese
queijo de Palmela, white, mild cheese
queijo Minas, cheese made of cow's milk. It is white, slightly salted
   and fat free
queijo Prato, mild, yellow cheese
queijo rabaçal, a goat's milk cheese
queijo requeijão, a type of cottage cheese
queijo São Jorge, similar to cheddar cheese
quente, hot
quente e frio, hot-fudge sundae
quiabo, okra
quibe, meat loaf dish from São Paulo
quibebe, pumpkin purée
rabada ensopada, oxtail stew
rabanada, french toast
rabanete, radish
raia, skate
ralado, grated
rebuçados, candy
receita, recipe
recheado, stuffed

ON A DOOR	
open – *aberto*	
closed – *fechado*	
entrance – *entrada*	
exit – *saída*	

45

recheio, stuffing
recheio de carne, meat filling
refeição, meal. *Refeicào para crianças* is
   a children's portion
refeição ligeira, snack
refogado, onions fried in olive oil
refresco, juice
refrigerante, soda
região, regional
remoulade, mustard and herb dressing
repolho, cabbage
requeijão, curd cheese
reserva, high quality aged wine
ricota, similar to Italian ricotta cheese
rillete, potted pork
rim, kidney
risol, deep-fried meat patties
robalo, sea bass
rodela, a round slice
rojões, fried pork
rolo de carne, meatloaf
rolos de couve lombarda, stuffed cabbage leaves
   (with sausage or minced meat inside)
romã, pomegranate
rosca, ring-shaped white bread
roupa velha, shredded beef in a tomato-based sauce
   (means "old clothes")
ruivo, red gurnard fish
safio, conger eel
sal, salt
salada, salad
salada de alface, green salad
salada de atum, tuna salad
salada de fruta, fruit salad
salada de macarrão, cold pasta salad
salada de ovos, egg salad
salada de palmito, salad made of palm shoots
salada mista, mixed salad
salada russa, cooked, diced vegetables and potatoes served in
   mayonnaise (Russian potato salad)
salame, salami
salgadinhos de bacalhau, cod mixed with mashed potatoes
   and deep fried
salgado, salty/salted
salmão, salmon
salmão fumado, smoked salmon
salmonete, mullet

ON THE TABLE	
spoon	*colher*
fork	*garfo*
knife	*faca*
napkin	*guardanapo*
glass	*copo*
salt	*sal*
pepper	*pimenta*
menu	*ementa*
candle	*vela*
plate	*prato*

salpicão, mixed salad which often contains slices of chicken. The salad dressing is usually creamy mayonnaise

salsa, parsley

salsicha, sausage

salsicha de coquetel, cocktail sausage

salsicha de peru, turkey sausage

salteado, sautéed

salva, sage

sande/sanduíche, sandwich

santola, spider crab

saquinho, bag. *Saquinho de chá* is a tea bag

sarda, mackerel

sardinha, sardine

saudades, dessert made of sugar, tapioca and egg yolks

sauté, sautéed

sável, shad

seco, dry/dried

seleção, selection. *Seleção de queijos* is a selection of cheeses

sem, without

sem gas, without carbonation

sem gelo, without ice

sêmola, semolina

sericá alentejano, cinnamon soufflé

serviço incluído, service included

siri, crab

siri recheado, crab shell stuffed with crabmeat, tomatoes, onions and peppers

sirva gelado, served chilled

sobremesa, dessert

solha, sole

sonho, a type of donut

sopa, soup

sopa à Alentejana, soup made using coriander, garlic browned in oil, bread and eggs

sopa de agriões, watercress and potato soup

sopa de beterraba, beet soup

sopa de cebola gratinada, fresh onion soup

sopa de coentros, soup with bread, poached eggs, coriander leaves, garlic and olive oil

sopa de feijão, soup with carrots, kidney beans, rice and cabbage

sopa de feijão preto, black bean soup

sopa de hortaliça, fresh vegetable soup

sopa de hortelã, mint soup

sopa de milho verde, green corn cob soup

sopa de palmito, cream of hearts-of-palm soup

sopa de panela, egg-based dessert

sopa de pedra, thick vegetable soup

sopa de rabo de boi, oxtail soup
sopa de siri, creamy crab soup
sopa de tartaruga, turtle soup
sopa de tomate à alentejana, soup with onions, tomatoes and
   poached eggs
sopa do dia, soup of the day
sopa e cozido, meat stew
sopa juliana, shredded vegetable soup
sopa leão velloso, seafood chowder
sopa transmontana, soup with ham, bacon, vegetables and bread
sorvete, ice-cream
sorvete com àgua, sherbet
sumo, juice
supremo de frango, boned and breaded chicken breast
sururu, a type of cockle
suspiro, meringue (means "sigh")
tacacá, soup of dried shrimp and tapioca
tainha, grey mullet fish
tâmara, date
tangerina, tangerine
tarifas de consumo, price list
tartaruga, turtle
tarte, tart/quiche
taxa de serviço, service charge
tempero, seasoning
tempero de salada, salad dressing
tenro, tender
tigelada, eggs beaten with milk and cinnamon
tinto, red
tixa aplicada, cover charge
tomar, soft fresh goat's cheese
tomate, tomato
tomilho, tender
toranja, grapefruit
tornedó, round cut of beef (tournedos)
torrada, toast.
torrado, toasted
torrão de ovos, marzipan
torresmos, fried pork fat and skin
torta, pie/tart/patty
tosta, toasted sandwich
tosta mista, toasted ham and cheese sandwich
tortilha, omelet
tortilha de mariscos, omelet filled with shellfish
toucinho, bacon
toucinho do céu, marzipan pudding
toucinho fumado, bacon

travesseiros, almond pastries
triga, wheat
tripas, tripe
tripas à moda do Porto, tripe cooked with assorted pork, chicken, vegetables and beans and served with rice
trouxas de ovos, sweetened egg yolks topped with syrup
trufa, truffle
truta, trout
turlu-furnu, baked eggplant, onions, potatoes and tomatoes
tutano, marrow
tutu à mineira/tutu mineiro, black beans mixed with cassava-root
uva, grape
uva passa, raisin
vaca, beef
vaca cozida, boiled beef
vaca estufada, beef stew
vapor, steamed
variado, assorted
veado, venison
vegitariano, vegetarian
velha, old, mature (as in liquor)
velhíssma, very old, mature liquor
vermute, vermouth
vieira, scallop
vinagre, vinegar
vinho, wine
vinho branco, white wine
vinho claro, unfortified wine
vinho da casa, house wine
vinho da Madeira, Madeira wine
vinho de mesa, table wine
vinho de Xerêz, sherry
vinho do Porto, port wine
vinho espumante, sparkling wine
vinho generoso, wine fortified with brandy
vinho moscatel, muscatel wine
vinho rosé, rosé wine
vinho spumoso, sparkling wine
vinho tinto, red wine
vinho verde, green wine made from unripened grapes. It is young, slightly sparkling and acidic. You drink it chilled
vitela, veal
viveiro de mariscos, seafood stew
yogurte, yogart

WINE	
red –	*vinho tinto*
white –	*vinho branco*
rose –	*vinho rosé*
corkscrew –	*saca-rolhas*
list –	*lista de vinhos*

Spanish Pronunciation Guide

If you are looking for a comprehensive guide to speaking Spanish, this is not the the right place. What follows are simply a few tips for speaking Spanish and a very brief pronunciation guide.

It is always good to learn a few polite terms so that you can excuse yourself when you've stepped on the foot of an elderly lady or spilled your drink down the back of the gentleman in front of you. It's also just common courtesy to greet the people you meet in your hotel, in shops and restaurants in their own language.

The Spanish language is actually very straightforward. Unlike English, every letter is pronounced in Spanish, even the final vowels on words ending with *e*'s. The one major exception is the double *l* which is pronounced like a *y* (tortilla) in Central and most of South America, or *sh,* in Spain and some parts of South America.

The last syllable is stressed in words ending with a consonant except *n* and *s*.

The next to the last syllable is stressed in words ending with *n* and *s* and in words ending in a vowel.

If a word is an exception to the above rules, an accent appears over the vowel of the stressed syllable.

a like *ah*
b usually the same as in English, but sometimes like a *v*
c similar to the English *k*
c before *e* and *i*, similar to the English *s* or *th* (in Spain)
ch the same as in English
d similar to the English d, except at the end of a word or between vowels, like th
e like e in they
f the same as in English
g like g in gate
g before *e* and *i*, like the English j

h not pronounced in Spanish

i like the English e

j like a throaty h

k the same as in English (and in words of foreign origin)

l the same as in English

ll like a *y* in Central and most of South America, like an *sh* in Spain and some of South America

m the same as English

n the same as English

ñ like a combination of *n* and *y* as in canyon

o like *oh*

p the same as English

q pronounced like a k

r pronounced like an *r* with the tip of the tongue against the ridge of the gums

rr a strong rolled r sound

s the same as English

t the same as English

u like the u in crude

v like the English *b*, except like the English *v* within a word

w the same as in English (and only found in words of foreign origin)

y the same as in English, except when alone like ee in meet. In Argentina and Uruguay like a combination of *j* and *z*

z like *th* in Spain and like *s* in all other Spanish-speaking countries

---

LET'S DRINK!	**TOP TAPAS!**
wine, *vino*	*tortilla española*, **omelette with potato and onion**
beer, *cerveza*	*jamón serrano*, **cured ham**
glass, *vaso*	*albóndigas*, **meatballs**
bottle, *botella*	*almendras*, **almonds**
cheers, *salud*	*mejillones*, **mussels**
wine list, *carta de vinos*	*gambas*, **shrimp**
wine (red), *vino tinto*	*chorizo*, **cured sausage**
wine (rosé), *vino rosado/rosé*	*olivas*, **olives**
wine (white), *vino blanco*	

English to Spanish

This is a brief listing of some familiar English foods and food-related words that you may need in a restaurant setting. It is followed by a list of phrases that may come in handy.

anchovy, anchoa
appetizer, una tapa
apple, manzana
artichoke, alcachofa
ashtray, cenicero
asparagus, espárragos
avocado, aguacate
bacon, tocino/beicon
baked, al horno
banana, banana. Do not confuse this with *plátano*
bean, judía/frijole/habichuela
beef, carne de vaca/buey
beef steak, bistec/biftec
beer, cerveza
beverage, bebida
bill, la cuenta
bitter, amargo
boiled, hervido
bottle (half), media botella
bottle, botella
bowl, tazón
bread roll, panecillo/pancito
bread, pan
breakfast, desayuno
broiled, asado
broth, caldo
butter, mantequilla
cabbage, repollo/col
cake, una torta/un pastel
candle, vela
carrot, zanahoria
cereal, cereal
chair, silla
check, la cuenta
cheers, salud

cheese, queso
cherry, cereza
chicken soup, caldo de gallina/sopa de pollo
chicken, pollo
chop, chuleta
clam, almeja
cocktail, aperitivo/cóctel
cod, bacalao
coffee, café
coffee with hot water (to dilute), café con agua caliente
coffee with milk, café con leche
coffee (black), café negro
coffee (decaf), café descafeinado
coffee (small cup) with milk or cream, café cortado
cold, frío
condiment, condimento
corn, maíz
cottage cheese, requesón
cover charge, cubierto
cucumber, pepino
cup, taza
demitasse/black coffee, café solo
dessert, postre
dinner, cena/comida
dish (plate), plato
drink, bebida
duck, pato
egg, huevo
espresso, café exprés
fish, pescado
fish soup, sopa de pescado
fork, tenedor

fowl, gallina
french fries, patatas fritas
fresh, fresco
fried, frito
fruit, fruta
game, carne de caza
garlic, ajo
gin, ginebra
glass, vaso
glass with stem, copa
goat (baby), cabrito
grape, uva
grapefruit, pomelo/toronja
green bean, judías verde
grilled, a la parilla/plancha
ham (boiled), lacón
ham (cured), jamón
hamburger, hamburguesa
honey, miel
hors d'oeuvre, entremeses
hot, caliente
ice, hielo
ice cream, helado
iced coffee, café granizado
iced tea, té helado
ice (on the rocks), con hielo
ice water, agua helada
ketchup, salsa de tomate
knife, cuchillo
lamb, cordero
large, grande
lemon, limón
lettuce, lechuga
little (a little), poco
liver, hígado
lobster, langosta
loin, lomo
lunch, almuerzo
mango, mango
marinated, escabeche
match, fósforo/cerilla
mayonnaise (with), alli olli

meat, carne
medium (cooked), regular/un
   poquito crudo
melon, melón
menu, la carta/el menú
milk, leche
mineral water, agua mineral
mineral water (sparkling),
   agua mineral gaseoso or
   con gas
mineral water (without
   carbonation), agua mineral
   sin gas
mixed, mixta
mushroom, seta/champiñon
mussel, mejillón
mustard, mostaza
napkin, servilleta
noodles, tallarines
octopus, pulpo
oil, aceite
olive oil, aceite de oliva
omelette, tortilla
on the rocks (with ice),
   con hielo
onion, cebolla
orange, naranja
orange juice, jugo de naranja
overdone, demasiado hecha
oyster, ostra
partridge, perdiz
pastry, pastel
peach, melocotón
pear, pera
pea, guisante
pepper (spice), pimienta
pepper (vegetable), pimiento
perch, mero
pineapple, piña
plantain, plátano
plate (dish), plato
please, por favor

plum, ciruela
poached, hervido
pork, cerdo/puerco
potato, patata
poultry, aves
prawn, gamba/langostinos
quail, codorniz
rabbit, conejo
rare, cruda/poco hecha
raspberry, frambuesa
receipt, recibo
rice, arroz
rice pudding, arroz con leche
roasted, asado
salad, ensalada
salt, sal
salty, salado
sandwich, sandwich, bocadillo
  or torta
sauce, salsa
saucer, platillo
sautéed, salteado
scallop, vieira
scrambled, revuelto
seafood, mariscos
seasoning, condimento
sherry, jerez
shrimp, camarón/gamba
small, pequeño
smoked, ahumado
snail, caracol
sole, lenguado
soup, sopa/caldo
sparkling (wine), espumoso
specialty, especialidad
spinach, espinaca
spoon, cuchara
squid, calamar
steak, filete
steamed, cocido al vapor
stewed, estofado
strawberry, fresa

sugar, azúcar
sugar substitute, sacarina
supper, cena
sweet, dulce
table, mesa
tea, té
tea with lemon, té con limón
tea with milk, té con leche
teaspoon, cucharilla
tenderloin, solomillo/filete
thank you, gracias
tip, propina
toasted, tostado
tomato, tomate
trout, trucha
tumbler (glass), vaso
tuna, atún/bonito
turkey, pavo
utensil, utensilio
veal, ternera
vegetable, legumbre/verdura
vegetarian, vegeteriano
venison, venado
vinegar, vinagre
vodka, vodka
waiter, camarero/señor
waitress, camarera/señora
  or señorita
water, agua
watermelon, sandía
well done, muy hecho/bien
  cocido
whipped cream, nata
wine, vino
wine (full-bodied), vino de
  cuerpo
wine list, carta de vinos
wine (red), vino tinto
wine (rosé), vino rosado/rosé
wine (white), vino blanco
yogurt, yogart

Helpful Phrases

please, por favor

thank you, gracias

a table, please, una mesa, por favor

I want to reserve a table, quiero reservar una mesa

for one person, para una persona

for two persons, para dos personas

    tres (3),

    cuatro (4),

    cinco (5),

    seis (6),

    siete (7),

    ocho (8),

    nueve (9),

    diez (10)

now, ahora

this evening, esta noche

tomorrow, mañana

the day after tomorrow, pasado mañana

near the window, cerca de la ventana

outside, a fuera

inside, dentro

on the patio, en el patio

on the balcony, en el balcón

with a view, con una vista

no smoking, no fumar

where is?, ¿donde esta?

the bathroom, el cuarto de baño (los servicios)

The bill please, la cuenta, por favor

a mistake (error), un error

Is service included?, ¿Está el servicio incluido? or ¿Está incluida la propina?

Do you accept credit cards?, ¿Aceptan tarjetas de crédito?

What is this?, ¿Qué es esto?

I did not order this, No pedí esto

This is, Esto está

too, demasiado

cold, fría/frío

spicy, picante

not fresh, no está fresco

not cooked, no está hecho

burnt, quemado

very good, muy bueno

delicious, delicioso or rico

cheap/expensive, barato(a)/caro(a)

good/bad, bueno(a)/malo(a)

less/more, menos/más

I am tipsy, Soy mareado

I am a vegetarian, Soy vegetariano(a)

I am allergic, Soy alérgico(a)

without meat, sin carne

without seafood, sin mariscos

without pork, sin cerdo

open, abierto

closed, cerrado

Monday, lunes

Tuesday, martes

Wednesday, miércoles

Thursday, jueves

Friday, viernes

Saturday, sábado

Sunday, domingo

Spanish to English

a caballo, steak topped with eggs (means "on horseback")
a punto, medium done
a su gusto, your own way
abadejo, fresh cod
aberezada, with dressing
aberezo de la mesa, condiments
abichón, sand smelt
abocado, semi-sweet table wine
abodado, marinated
acedera, sorrel
acedia, baby sole
aceite, oil
aceite de girosol, sunflower oil
aceite de oliva, olive oil
aceite de palma, palm oil
aceite de soja, soy-bean oil
aceituna, olive
aceituna negra, black olive
aceituna verde, green olive
aceitunas aliñadas, olives with salad dressing
aceitunas rellenas, stuffed olives
acelga, beet greens/beets/Swiss chard
acerola, wild cherry
achicoria, chicory/endive
achiote, annatto-seed paste
aderezo (de mesa), condiments
adobadas, pickled
adobo, marinated prior to cooking.
    This can also refer to marinated fried fish
adobos de carne, meat marinades
agridulce, sweet and sour
agua, water
aguacate, avocado
agua de azahar, orange- or lemon-blossom water
agua de coca, coconut water
agua de grifo, tap water
agua de panela, drink made from water and sugar
agua de sel, seltzer or soda water
agua destilada, distilled water
agua dulce, boiled water with brown sugar
agua fresca, sweet, water-based beverage flavored with fruit
agua helada, ice water
agua mineral, mineral water

Aceite, the word for oil, is derived from Aceituna, the word for olive.

Spain is the world's largest producer of olives.

agua mineral con gas, mineral water (sparkling)
agua mineral gaseoso, mineral water (sparkling)
agua mineral sin gas, mineral water (without carbonation)
agua potable, drinking water
agua purificado/agua puro, purified water
aguardiente, strong liqueur made from the pressings of grape skins. In
    Latin America, sugar-cane or corn-based liquor
aguja, needlefish/sparkling beverage
agujas, en, on skewers
ahumado, smoked
ahumados variados, smoked fish
aigua, the Catalan word for water
ajada, garlic and oil sauce
ajedrea, savory
ajetes, garlic shoots
ají, chili, red pepper
ají de gallina, shredded chicken in a cream
    and pepper sauce
ajiaceite, garlic oil/garlic mayonnaise
ajiaco bogotano, thick potato soup (frequently with chicken)
ajilla, garlic sauce
ajillo, cooked in garlic and oil
ajillo moruno, Moorish casserole of bread, almonds, chopped beef or
    liver, garlic and seasonings
ajo, al, contains whole garlic cloves
ajo, garlic
ajo arriero, with garlic, paprika and parsley
ajo blanco, cold almond and garlic soup
ajocabañil, meat prepared with vinegar, garlic and paprika
ajo de Mataero, dish of bacon, liver and pork
ajonjolí, sesame seed
ajopollo, chicken with garlic and almond sauce
al, a la, with/in the style of
aladroc, anchovies
alajú, cake with honey and almonds
alas, wings
albacora, swordfish
albahaca, basil
albardado, in a batter
albaricoque, apricot
albariño, al, in a white-wine sauce
albariño, white wine
albóndigas, meatballs/fishballs
albufera, sauce with red pepper, almonds and cream
alcachofa, artichoke
alcachofas a la andaluza, artichokes with bacon and ham
alcaparra, caper

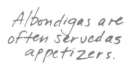

Handwritten margin notes:

Aguardiente, like white lightening, has an extremely high alcohol content.

Ajo

Albacora.

Albóndigas are often served as appetizers.

57

alcapurias, ground plantains with fish or meat fried in batter
alcaravea, caraway seed
alcohólica, alcoholic beverage
alfajores, small round cakes
algar-robina, *pisco* and carob syrup
alicantina, a la, with green peppers, artichokes and seafood
aliñada, marinated or seasoned or with salad dressing
aliño, dressing
alioli/ali oli/all-i-oli, garlic mayonnaise/garlic purée
allada, garlic and oil sauce
ali-pebre/all-i-pebre, garlic, oil and paprika sauce
almadrote, sauce with garlic, cheese and eggplant
almejas, clams
almejas a la buena mujer, clams in a wine and parsley sauce
almejas a la marinera, clams in a white sauce
almejas al natural/almejas naturales, live clams
almendrada, cooked with almonds
almendras, almonds
almendras garrapiñadas, sugar-coated toasted almonds
almendras saladas, salted almonds
almendras tostadas, toasted almonds
almíbar, syrup
almojábanas, syrup-coated buns/corn muffins
almuerzo, lunch
aloque, red wine (made from a mixture of white and red grapes)
alpargata, sweet biscuit
alubias, kidney beans/broad beans/fava beans
alvocat, the Catalan word for avocado
amanida, salad with fish and meat
amargo, bitter
amarilla, en, sauce with saffron and onions
amarillos (en dulce), ripe (yellow) plantains fried in a red wine, sugar
    and cinnamon sauce
amontillado, medium-dry sherry, older than *jerez fino,* aged at least
    eight years in wood
anacardos, cashews
anafre, bean paste smothered with melted cheese
ananás, pineapples
ancas de rana, frog legs
ancho, dried *poblano* pepper
anchoas, anchovies
anchoas a la barquera, anchovies with capers
andalucía, dry sherry and orange juice
andaluza, a la, with red peppers, tomatoes and garlic
ánec, the Catalan word for duck
añejo, aged
angélica, liquor similar to yellow Chartreuse
58

A la buena mujer means of the good woman

Alubias blancas are white beans rojas are red, rosadas, pink

Ancas de rana

angelote, angelfish

anguila, eel

angula, baby eel

anís, anise/anise-flavored liquor

anisado, anise-flavored soda

anís seco, anise-flavored beverage

añojo, veal

anona, custard apple

anticucho, beef kebabs

antojito, *tortilla* sandwich filled with beef, tomatoes and onions/snack

anxova, the Catalan word for anchovy

aperitivo, cocktail/aperitif

api, drink made from corn and cinnamon

apio, celery

arandano, cranberry

arencas, salted sardines

arenque, herring

arenque en escabeche, pickled herring

arepa, corn-meal pancake or muffin

armañac, a type of brandy made from *aguardiente*

aromáticas, herbal teas

arroces, rice dishes

arrope, honey syrup

arròs, rice dish/soup with rice. ***Arròs en cassola*** is a dish of rice
with assorted seafood from *Costa Brava*. ***Arròs negre*** is a squid
and rice dish from *Catalonia*

arroz, rice

arroz a la banda, fish and rice with saffron

arroz a la catalana, rice with peppers and sausage

arroz a la Cubana, rice with tomato
sauce, fried egg and banana

arroz a la emperatriz, rice with apricots,
raisins, truffles, milk and Cointreau

arroz a la española, rice with chicken
livers, pork and tomatoes

arroz a la mexicana, a blend of tomatoes, rice and onions

arroz a la valenciana, rice with chicken, vegetables and shellfish

arroz a la vasca, rice with chicken giblets

arroz al canario, rice with ham and bananas

arroz al caldo, consommé with rice

arroz blanco, boiled, steamed rice

arroz brut, dry soup (see ***sopas secas***) of rice and meats

arroz caldoso, rice soup

arroz con cacao, chocolate-flavored rice pudding

arroz con coco y titi, rice with coconut and shrimp

arroz con costra, rice (*paella*) with meatballs

arroz con dulce, sweet rice pudding

anguila

Anticucho is often beef heart.

Apio

Armañac

Arroz a la Cubana
is sometimes
made with banana
instead of
Tomato.

arroz con habichuelas, rice and beans
arroz con leche, rice pudding
arroz con mariscos, rice with seafood
arroz con pollo, rice and chicken
arroz en caldero, rice with red peppers and seafood
arroz empedrat, rice with beans and tomatoes
arroz escarlata, rice with shrimp and tomatoes
arroz marinera, rice with assorted seafood
arroz moro, rice with spicy meat
arroz negro, rice made black by cooking in squid ink
arroz primavera, rice with vegetables
arvejas, peas
asadillo, roasted, skinned peppers with garlic
asado, roasted/roasted meats
asado de tira, spareribs
asador, grill room, rotisserie
asadurilla, lamb's liver stew
asopao, a thick stew made with rice and with meat or seafood
asturias, sharp-flavored cheese
ata, whipped cream
atole, oat-based beverage
atún, tuna
auyama, a fruit similar to pumpkin
avellana, hazelnuts
avena, oats. Can also refer to oatmeal
aves, poultry
aviram, The Catalan word for poultry
azafrán, saffron
azahar, orange blossom
azúcada, sugared
azúcar, sugar
azúcar de acre, maple syrup
azúcar demerara, granulated brown sugar
azúcar enpolvo/azúcar glace, powdered sugar
azúcar moreno, brown sugar
babarrúa de naranja, frozen orange custard
bacalao/balcallao, salt cod
bacalao a la catalana, cod with ham, parsley, garlic and almonds
bacalao al ajo arriero, cod with parsley, garlic and peppers
bacalao a la riojana, cod and sauce with paprika and peppers
bacalao a la vizcaína, cod with ham, peppers, tomato sauce
    and potatoes
bacalao pil-pil, cod casserole with garlic and oil
bacalitos (fritos), fried cod fritters
bacallà, the Catalan word for cod
bacon, bacon
baho, tomato and beef stew

Asopao is Puerto Rico's most popular dish.

atun.

bajoques farcides, meat and rice stuffed in red peppers
baleadada, *tortilla* filled with cheese, beans and eggs
banda de almendra, almond-and-marmalade puff pastry
bandarillo/banderillo, small skewer with ham, cheese or pickle
bandeja, de, tray of (as in tray of cheeses)
bandeja paisa, main dish. In Colombia this is a dish with ground beef,
   sausage, salt pork, beans, rice, avocado and fried egg.
   This dish is also called *plato montañero*
barbacoa, barbecued
barbo, barbel (a fresh-water fish)
barcoretta, tuna
barquillos, small cookies
barra, bar (as in a chocolate bar)
bartolillos, deep-fried pastry filled with custard
batata, sweet potato
batida/batido, milk shake
baveresa de coco, cold coconut dessert
bayas, berries
bebidas, beverages
bebidas alcohólicas, alcoholic beverages
bebidas refrescantes, soft drinks
becada, woodcock
beicon, bacon
ben fet, the Catalan expression for well-done
berberecho, tiny clams found in Cantabria
berenjena, eggplant/aubergine
berenjena de Almagro, pickled eggplant
berenjena rebozada, battered and fried sliced eggplant
berenjenas a la mallorquina, eggplants with garlic mayonnaise
berraza, parsnip
berros, watercress
bertón, stuffed cabbage
berza, cabbage
besugo, sea bream/porgy
besugo a madrileña, baked bream with lemon and oil
besugo asado con piriñaca, bream baked with red peppers
besugo mechado, bream stuffed with bacon and ham
beterragas, sweet potatoes
bicarbonato de sosa, baking soda
bien cocido, well-done
bien hecho, well-done
bien-me-sabe coco, cake with coconut-cream topping
bien pasado, well-done
bife, steak
bife a lo pobre, large steak with fried potatoes and onions, served with
   two fried eggs on top
bife de lomo, T-bone steak served without the bone

Barra de Pan is a loaf of Bread.

Batata blanca is sweet potato with pink skin and yellow flesh.

Bien me sabe means I know it does me good.

61

biftec, beef steak
biftek de ternera/bistek de ternera, veal steak
biftec encebollado, steak with fried onions
biftek salteado al jerez, fried steak with sherry
bis/bisso, chub (mackerel)
bistek, beef steak
bizcocho, spongecake dessert
bizcochos borrachos, spongecake soaked in liquor (usually rum)
    and/or syrup
bizcotela, cookie
blanco y negro, iced milk, coffee and cinnamon
blando, soft
blanquillos, eggs
bocadillo, snack/sandwich usually with ham and cheese
bocadillos de monja (nun's mouthful), cake with egg, sugar
    and almonds
bocas, small appetizers served with alcoholic beverages
bodega, wine or sherry cellar
bogovante/bogavante, lobster
boletos, cepe/porcini mushrooms
bolillos, sandwich bread rolls
bolitas, cheese balls
bollito, bread roll/bun
bollo, bread roll/bun/breakfast roll baked with sugar
bollo de panizo, scone made of corn meal
bollo escocés, scone
bollo preñado, roll filled with meat
bollos de maíz, deep-fried corn puffs
bomba, meatball with chili sauce
bomba helada, baked Alaska
bombón, bonbon
boniato, similar, but not related, to a yam. Sometimes called a
    Cuban sweet potato
bonito, tuna
boquerones, anchovies. A popular first course in Spain
boquitas, small appetizers such as olives, peanuts or crackers
bori-bori, chicken soup with corn-meal balls
borona, corn meal
borra, cod, spinach and potato soup
borracho, grey gurnard (seafood)
borrachos, cakes soaked in wine or syrup
botella, bottle
botella media, half bottle
botellín, small bottle of beer
bou, the Catalan word for beef
bover, snail
brandada de bacalao, creamy cod purée

62

brasa, barbecued/grilled
braseado/a, braised
brazo de gitano, spongecake roll with custard filling
breca, a type of sea bream
brécol, broccoli

Brazo de gitano means gypsy arm.

brevas, deep-fried doughnuts with custard filling. In Latin America, this refers to figs
bróccolis/bróculi, broccoli
brochetas, en, on skewers
broquil, broccoli
brotes, bean sprouts
brut, extremely dry wine
budín, pudding/custard

Not the budin found in creole countries which is blood sausage and is called ButiFarra iN Latin America.

buey, beef
buey de mar, large-clawed crab
buey estofado, beef stew with potatoes, sausage and wine
buñuelo, fried pastry/doughnut
buñuelo de bacalao, fried pastry with dried, salted cod
buñuelo de cuaresma rellenos, fried pastry with chocolate and cream
buñuelo de San Isidro, fried dessert pastry with sesame seeds and anise
buñuelo de viento, dessert of fried doughnuts with syrup
bunyettes, doughnuts
burgos, fresh, creamy white cheese
burrito, stuffed *tortilla*
búsano, whelk (seafood)
buseca, spicy oxtail soup. A specialty in Uruguay
butifarra, spiced sausage made of pork and/or veal. In Latin America, spicy blood sausage
buvangos rellenos, stuffed zucchini
caballa, mackerel
cabello de ángel, stewed sweet pumpkin or squash
cabeza de cerdo, brawn

Cabeza de Cerdo is a fish but the name means Pig's head.

cabeza de ternera, seasoned veal loaf/calf's head
cabra, goat. This can also refer to a spider crab in Catalonia
cabracho, scorpion fish
cabrales, a creamy blue cheese
cabrillo, comber (seafood)
cabrito, goat (kid)
cabrito asado roasted kid
cacao, cocoa
cacahuetes, peanuts
cacereña, black olive
cacerola, casserole
cachelada, potato and sausage stew
cachelos, diced, boiled potato dish
cachito, croissant
café, coffee

café americano, black coffee (diluted)
café am llet, The Catalan phrase for coffee with milk
café con agua caliente, coffee with hot water (to dilute)
café con hielo, iced coffee
café con leche coffee with milk
café cortado, small cup of coffee with a small amount of milk or cream
café de olla, coffee with cinnamon and sugar
café descafeinado, decaffeinated coffee
café doble, large cup of coffee
café exprés, espresso
café grande, large cup of coffee
café granizado, iced coffee
café guayoyo, large cup of mild, black coffee
café irlandés, Irish coffee
café marrón, large cup of strong coffee with a small amount of milk
café marroncito, small cup of strong coffee
    with a small amount of milk
café negrito, small cup of strong black coffee
café negro, black coffee
café perfumado, coffee with milk
café perico, coffee with liquor (usually brandy)
café solo, demitasse/black coffee
cafetería, self-service cafeteria
café tinto, black coffee
café vienés, black coffee and whipped cream
caguama, turtle
cailón, shark
caimito, star-shaped apple
calabacín (or calabacita), zucchini
calabaza, pumpkin
calamares, squid
calamares a la romana, fried squid
calamares en su tinta, squid cooked in its own ink
calamares fritos, deep-fried squid
calamaritos, baby squid
calamarsos, the Catalan word for squid
calcots, spring onions
calda/caldo, hot
caldeirada, stew
caldera de dátiles de mar, seafood stew
caldereta, stew
caldereta asturiana, seafood stew
caldereta de cordero a la pastora, lamb and vegetable stew
caldereta de gallega, vegetable stew
caldereta de ternera, potted veal roast
caldero, cauldron
caldillo, clear fish soup

Cafe Irlandés

calamares

64

caldillo de congrio, conger-eel soup with potatoes and tomatoes
caldillo de perro, hake soup
caldo/calda, hot
caldo, broth/consommé
caldo de, soup
caldo de gallina, chicken soup
caldo de pescado, fish soup
caldo de res, beef stock and vegetable soup
caldo gallego, meat and vegetable soup (frequently ham and cabbage)
caldo guanche, soup with potatoes, tomatoes, onions, and zucchini
caldo verde, cabbage-based broth with potato and greens
caliente, hot. Often refers to a dish with a hot chili sauce
callampas, mushrooms
callos, tripe
callos a la catalana, tripe stew with wine and pine nuts
callos a la madrileña, tripe stew with peppers, sausage,
    ham and tomatoes
camarera, waitress
camarero, waiter
camarones, shrimp
camarones a la plancha, shrimp marinated and then grilled
camarones del rio, freshwater crayfish
camote, sweet potato
caña, mug of draft beer/alcoholic beverage from Paraguay made from
    sugar cane and similar to rum
caña de dulce, sugar cane
caña de vaca, marrow bone
cañadilla/cañailla, snail
canas, pastry cones filled with custard or cream
canela, cinnamon
canelones, cannelloni
canelones a la barcelonesa, ham and chicken-liver stuffed cannelloni
cangrejo (de mar), crab
cangrejo (de río), crayfish (river crab)
canilla, snack
canitas, pastry cones filled with custard or cream
cantarela, chanterelle mushroom
canutillos, custard-filled pastry horns topped
    with cinnamon and powdered sugar
capirotada, meat dish in an almond sauce
capitán, *pisco* and vermouth
capitón, grey mullet
caqui, persimmon
carabineros, large shrimp
caracoles, snails. *Caracoles de carne* are meat-filled buns
carajillo, coffee with brandy
carajillo de ron, coffee with rum

callampas.

Camarones.

cantarella.

65

carajillo de vodka, coffee with vodka *Carajillo can also be served with Anisette.*

carajitos, hazelnut macaroons

carambola, starfruit

caramelo, caramel

caraotas, beans

carbón, any charcoal-grilled filling

carbonada, beef stew, usually with rice, sweet potatoes, squash, apples and peaches (baked in a pumpkin shell); also called *carbonada criollo*

Carbonada is the Argentine version of Belgian Carbonade

carbonada de buey, beef cooked in beer

carbonero, coalfish (cod)

cardamomo, cardamom

cardo, cardoon

cargol, snail

cari, curry

cargol.

carimañolas, turnover filled with cheese or meat

carne, meat

carne a la parilla, grilled steak

carne alambres, meat on a skewer

carne asada, grilled meat/barbecued beef

carne asada a la tampiqueña, beef steak with guacamole and beans

carne asada al horno, roast meat

carne de buey, beef

carne de caza, game

carne de cerdo, pork

carne de chancho, pork

carne de lidia, very tough beef

carne de mebrillo, quince jelly

carne de res, beef

carne de res con chile colorado, beef in red chile

carne de vaca, beef

carne en salsa, meat in tomato sauce

carne guisada, sauce with stewed beef

carne mechada, a beef roast served with onions, ham and spices

carne molida, ground beef

carne para asar, beef roast

carne picada, ground meat

carnero, mutton

carnero verde, mutton dish with parsley and mint

carnitas, barbecued pork

carpa, carp

carquinyolis, almond biscuit

carrillada, pig cheek

carro de queso, cheese platter

carpa.

carta, la, menu

carta de vinos, wine list

Camarero, una carta por favor!

cártamo, safflower

66

casa, de la, of the house, could mean *specialty* or *homemade*
casadiellas, dessert turnovers
casados, fish, meat or chicken with rice, beans and vegetables
cáscara, rind/zest/peel/shell
casero, homemade
casi crudo, very rare
castañas, chestnuts
castellana, bread and garlic soup
castoñola, sea perch

castoñola

catalana, a la, cooked in a tomato sauce
causa a la limeña, potato pureé with shrimp salad.
 A specialty from Peru
cava, sparkling wine
caza, game
cazadora, a la, with mushrooms, onions and herbs
cazón, dogfish/shark
cazón en adobo, shark marinated
 in vinegar, paprika, cumin and oregano;
 floured and deep-fried

a la cazadora.

cazuela, stew/casseroled. This also refers to a Puerto Rican pumpkin-
 and-coconut pudding
cazuela de ave, casserole with beans, corn, rice, pumpkin, carrots and
 spices. A specialty of Chile
cazuela de cordero, lamb stew with vegetables
cazuela de chichas, meat casserole
cazuelita, small casserole
ceba, the Catalan word for onion
cebada, barley
cebiche, see *ceviche*
cebolla, onion
cebollada, onion soup
cebolletas, scallions/chives
cebollinos, chives
cebrero, a creamy blue cheese
cecina, beef jerky/strip steak
cena, dinner/supper
cenicero, ashtray
centeno, rye bread
centollo, spider crab
centollo relleno, spider crab cooked in its shell
cepa, wine grape
cerdo, pork
cereales, cereals
cerezas, cherries
cerveza, beer
cerveza de barril/cerveza de presión, draft beer
cerveza dorada, light (in color, not necessarily in calories) beer

Cazuela is actually the name of the earthenware dish in which it is cooked.

Cerveza nationale is domestic beer and cerveza importada is imported beer. In case you couldn't figure that out.

cerveza extranjera, imported beer
cerveza negra, dark beer
cervecería, bar
césar/ensalada césar, Caesar salad
cesta de frutas, selection of fruit
ceviche, raw seafood marinated in lemon and lime juice; frequently served as an appetizer

chabacano, apricot
chacina, ground sausage
chacoli, Basque white wine
chairo, lamb broth with *chuños* and vegetables. A Bolivian specialty
chajá, spongecake, cream and jam dessert
chalote, chalotas, shallots
chalupa, deep-fried *tortilla* with many fillings
champaña/champán, champagne
champiñon, mushroom
chancetes, deep-fried small fish similar to whitebait
chancho, pork
chanfaina, pig stew with rice and blood sausage
chanfaina castellana, rice and sheep's-liver stew
changurro, Basque dish of seasoned crabmeat
chanquetes, deep-fried small fish similar to whitebait
chapin, trunkfish (found in Puerto Rico)

Chalupa, wh actually mea boat, is nam for the bo Shape of th finished tortilla.

chato, glass of red wine
chauchas, green beans
chayote, pear-shaped vegetable similar to squash
cherna, grouper
chica, alcoholic beverage of fermented grapes and juice
chica de jora, alcoholic beverage made from corn. The non-alcoholic version is ***chica morada***
chica de manzana, apple brandy
chicha, an alcoholic beverage made from corn

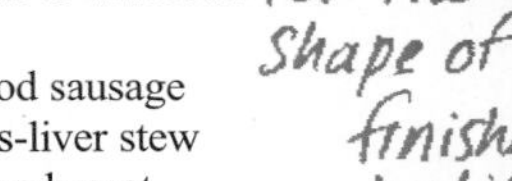

chicharos, peas
chicharro, mackerel
chicharrones, pork fat/fried pork rinds/fried pork skin
chicharrones de pollo, crispy fried chicken pieces
chichicuilotes, small sparrows boiled live, served stuffed with avocado

you may want to avoid this dish considering its grim preparation method.

chico zapote, the tropical fruit sapodilla found in Mexico
chifa, Chinese food
chilaquiles, pieces of fried *tortillas* with onions, red peppers, cheese and sour cream
chilcano, *pisco* and ginger ale
chile, chili pepper. Sweet to horribly hot and all shapes and colors! The Scoville scale

ranks the fire power of a
chili pepper. The hottest is a *habañero*
with a measure of 100,000 to 300,000 units.
In comparison, a *jalapeño* has a rank
of 2500-5000 units

chiles.

chile poblano, green pepper

chiles en nogada, green peppers stuffed
with whipped cream and nuts

chiles rellenos, stuffed peppers

chili, chili

chilindrón, refers to the use of red peppers and tomatoes in a dish.
For example, ***pollo chilindrón*** is a dish of chicken
with red peppers

chillo, red snapper

chiltepe, a chili of medium heat with a somewhat nutty flavor

chimichanga, deep-fried *tortilla* stuffed with beef, beans and chilies

chimichurri, barbecue sauce of tomatoes, garlic, onions

china, a sweet orange

chinola, passion fruit

chipas, bread made of corn flour, cheese and eggs

chipi chipi, clam soup

chipiron.

chipirón, small squid

chipotle, dark chili sauce/a smoked *jalapeño* pepper

chiquito, glass of red wine

chirimoyas, custard apple

chirivias, parsnips *The less said about parsnips ...*

chirmol, hot sauce made of onions, tomatoes and mint

chistorra, a narrow sausage with paprika

chivito, steak sandwich

chivito al plato, steak topped with a fried egg and served with potato
salad, a green salad and french fries

chivo, goat, kid

choclo, pastel de, a corn casserole filled with a variety of meats
and vegetables. This can also refer to corn on the cob

*Chocolate is native
to South America.*

chocolate, chocolate

chocolate caliente, hot chocolate.
Chocolate a la española is a thick hot chocolate drink

chocolate churros y porras, extremely popular fried pastry. ***Churros***
are loops and ***porras*** are sticks of deep-fried batter and are often
eaten at breakfast or bedtime with a cup of hot chocolate

chocolate con leche, hot chocolate milk

chocolate santafereño, hot chocolate and cheese

chocolatina, chocolate bar/candy bar

chocolate
caliente.

chocos, large squid/cuttlefish

cholga, giant mussels

chongos, cheese in a sweet syrup

chop, beer (usually draft beer)

chopa, a type of sea bream
chopitos, cuttlefish
choricero, chili
choripán, sausage baked in dough
choritos, small mussels
chorizo, cured sausage seasoned with
    paprika and garlic, almost always pork
    sausage. In Mexico, the sausage is
    usually made from fresh ground pork

During the Inquisition, a chorizo hung in the kitchen indicated th[at] a christian lived there.

chorizo de olla, sausage stew
choros, mussels
choto, baby goat. *Choto ajillo* is kid in a garlic casserole
chuchitos, meat and sauce in dough and wrapped in a corn husk
chuchuco, barley, meat and peppercorn soup
chucrut, sauerkraut
chufa, tiger nut
chufle, an alcoholic beverage from Bolivia made with *singani,* lemon
    juice and soda
chuleta, cutlet/chop
chuleta de cerdo a la asturiana, pork chop with apples in cider sauce
chuleta de gamo, venison
chuletita/chuletilla, small cutlet/small chop
chuletón, rib beef chop/large chop
chumbera/chumbo, prickly pear
chuños, freeze-dried potatoes from
    Bolivia and Peru
    (frequently mixed with meat, eggs or fish)
chupe de camarones, shrimp stew. *Chupe de mariscos* is seafood stew
chupete, sucker/lollipop

chumberas.

churisco, baked sausage
churrasco, grilled steak (usually a thin slice)
churros, loops of deep-fried batter often eaten with a cup of
    hot chocolate
cidra, squash/squash boiled in sugar
cidracayote de verano, summer squash
cierva, deer
cigala, prawn
cigalas cocidas, boiled prawns (sometimes lobster)
cigarra de mer, (clawless) lobster
cigron, the Catalan word for chickpea
cilantro, cilantro/coriander. This herb is used heavily in Mexico
cincho, hard cheese made from sheep's milk
ciruela, plum
ciruelas pasas/ciruelas secas, prunes
civet de liebre, marinated rabbit
clara, beverage made from a mixture of beer and lemonade
clara de huevo, egg white

clarete, light red wine/rosé wine
claro, light (in color)
clavo, clove
clementina, mandarin orange
clérico, wine and fruit juice
clima, al, at room temperature
clòssa, the Catalan word for clam
coca, pie
coca amb pinxes, sardine pie
coca mallorquina, similar to a pizza
cocadas/cocados, coconut cakes
cocarois, similar to a pizza and topped with raisins and pine nuts
cochifrito, milk-fed lamb stew
cochifrito de cordero, highly seasoned lamb stew
cochinillo, suckling pig *Cochinello.*
cochinillo asado, roasted suckling pig
cochinita, chopped pork dish
cocido, cooked, boiled, simmered. Can also refer to stew
cocido al vapor, steamed
cocido castellano, thick stew with sausage, chickpeas, chicken, bacon, potatoes and other vegetables
cocido con leche, *maté* with milk
cocido envuelto, baked in parchment
cocido madrileño, (Madrid stew) stew made from meat, vegetables and chickpeas
cocina casera, home cooking
coco, coconut
coco loco, coconut-flavored alcoholic beverage from Mexico
cocoa, chocolate
cococas, pieces of hake gills. See *kokotxas*
cocos, coconut cakes
cocos frios, chilled coconuts, tops chopped off, drunk with a straw. A specialty in Puerto Rico and the Dominican Republic
cóctel, cocktail
cóctel campechana marinera, oyster and shrimp cocktail
cóctel de camarón/cóctel de gamba, shrimp cocktail
cóctel de mariscos, seafood cocktail
codillo de cerdo, pig's feet
codoñate, quince, chestnut and honey cake
codoñate de nueces, walnut cake
codorniz (codornices), quail
codorniz al nido, quail in a "nest" of fried potatoes
codorniz en zurrón, quail in green peppers
cogollo de palmito, hearts of palm
cohombro, cucumber
col, cabbage
col de Bruselas, Brussels sprout

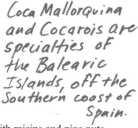

Coca Mallorquina and Cocarois are specialties of the Balearic Islands, off the Southern coast of Spain.

Cocos frios.

Cohombro.

71

cola, tail/oxtail

cola de mono, coffee, rum, milk and *pisco*.
In Chile, this is *aguardiente*,
coffee, sugar, milk, cinnamon and egg yolk. Similar to eggnog

colecillas de Bruselas, Latin American expression for Brussels sprouts

coles, cabbage leaves

coliflor, cauliflower

coliflor con bechamel, cauliflower and cheese

collejas, corn salad

colmenilla, morel mushrooms

comedor, dining room. You get a basic, inexpensive meal here. These
eating establishments have become harder to find

comida, lunch/meal

comida corrida, is a fixed-price menu in Mexico and
comida corriente is a fixed-priced menu in Central America

comino, cumin (used in Mexican chili powders)

compota, compote/stewed fruit

completo, hot dog

Completo

con, with. Often, this is abbreviated as *c/*

con hielo, beverage served "on the rocks"

coñac, brandy/cognac

concentrado, concentrate. *Concentrado
de tomate* is tomato paste

concha, conch

conchas finas, large scallops/Venus clam

conchas peregrinas, scallops

conchitas, the Peruvian word for scallops

Conchas finas.

condimentos, condiments/seasonings

conejo, rabbit

conejo del monte, wild rabbit

confitura, jam

congrio, conger eel

conill, the Catalan word for rabbit

conserva, pickled

congrio.

consomé/consumado, clear soup (frequently chicken broth)

consomé a la reina, consommé with egg

consomé de chivo, goat soup   *not a favorite*

contra de ternera, veal stew

contrafilete de ternera, veal fillet

copa, glass

copa de helado, assorted ice creams served in a glass

copa nuria, egg whipped and served with jam

copetin, in Uruguay, any alcoholic beverage served with appetizers

copitas, sherry glass

coques/coquetes, flat bread, frequently used for pizza dough

coquinas, clams

coquito, holiday coconut eggnog with rum. A Puerto Rican specialty

corazón, heart/core. This is also the Puerto Rican
  word for a custard apple
corazón de alcachofa, artichoke heart
corazón de palma, hearts of palm
corazonada, hearts stewed in sauce
cordero, lamb
cordero al chilindrón, lamb with red peppers
cordero lechal asado, roast lamb
cordero mamón, suckling lamb

Cordero.

cordero recental, spring lamb
cortadillo, small pancake with lemon
cortado, coffee with a dash of milk
corto, glass of draft beer

corto.

corvina, white sea bass
corzo, deer
cosecha, vintage. *Cosechero* is the latest vintage of red wine
costada, flank
costellada, grilled lamb chops

costrada
chocolate.

costilla, chop/spareribs
costilla de cerdo con poco carne, spareribs
costra, crust

costrada, slice of cake or pastry
costrada navarra, thick soup topped with a bread crust
cranc, the Catalan word for crab
cranc verd, shore crab
crema, cream, mousse, or purée (soup). Can refer to sour cream
  in Mexico
crema batida, whipped cream
crema catalana, crème caramel
cremada, dessert made from
  sugar, milk and eggs

Crème caramel, also
called flan, is
popular in all Spanish
speaking countries.

crema de arroz, creamy rice pudding
crema de cacao, chocolate liquor
crema de café, coffee liquor
crema de maranja, curaçao, an orange-flavored cordial
crema de menta, crème de menthe
crema de San José, chilled custard
cremadina, custard filling
crema española, milk, eggs and fruit-jelly dessert
crema nieve, frothy egg-yolk, sugar, rum or wine beverage
cremas, sweet liquors
cremat, coffee with rum and brandy
cremat, cooked to golden brown
crepa/crep/crepe, crêpe. *Crepe imperial* is a crêpe suzette
criadillas, testicles/sweetbreads
criadillas de la tierra, truffles

Thanks, but No
thanks.

crianza, wine aged in wood barrels

criolla, island cuisine that blends European, African, Taino and Arawak Indian foods *That's Creole to us.*

criolla, a la, with green peppers, tomatoes and spices

crocante, ice cream with chopped nuts

croquetas, fish, meat or vegetable croquettes. This can also refer to breaded and deep-fried pieces of chicken, pork or beef, a specialty of Paraguay

cru de peix, fish stew with raw or slightly cooked fish

crudo, raw

cuajada, cream-based dessert with honey

cuarto, roast/joint

cubalibre, rum and coca-cola

cubana, a la, with eggs and fried bananas

cubano, sandwich made of ham, chicken and/or pork, Swiss cheese, mustard and pickles

Cuba Lib

cubata, liquor mixed with a soft drink

cubierto, cover charge

cubito de hielo, ice cube

cubra libre, rum and coca-cola. Sometimes this is gin and coca cola

cucaracha, *tequila* and coffee-flavored alcoholic beverage

cuchara, spoon

cuchifrito, a stew of pork innards found in the Dominican Republic and Puerto Rico

cuchillo, knife

cuello, neck

cuenta, la, check/bill

cuerpo, de, full-bodied alcoholic beverage

cuitlacoche, a type of mushroom from Latin America

culantro, cilantro/coriander

curanto, A Chilean dish of meat (often suckling pig), vegetables and seafood

Curí? Thanks but we'll pass. Pass on the cusuco, too.

curí, grilled guinea pig. A Colombian dish

cusuco, armadillo

cuy, grilled guinea pig. A Colombian dish

damasco, apricot

dátil, date

dátiles de mar, shellfish

de, of

delicias, small spongecake

delicias de queso, breaded and deep-fried cheese

dentón, dentex (a type of bream)

desayuno, breakfast

descafeinado, decaffeinated

despojos, innards (offal)

destornillador, "screwdriver": vodka and orange juice

desayuno en la mañana

diablo, al, spicy tomato sauce
día, del, "of the day"
diente de ajo, clove of garlic
doble, a large glass of beer
donastiarra, a la, charcoal grilled
dorada, sea bream/dolphin
duelos y quebrantos, scrambled eggs, ham and sausage
dulce, sweet/sweet wine
dulce de batata, thick slices of sweet potatoes. A specialty in Argentina

> DOC on a wine label stands for *Denominacíon de Origen Calificada* and means the wine is from a high-quality producing area. DO stands for *Denominacion de Origen* and means the wine is a lower quality than DOC.

dulce de leche, milk simmered with vanilla and sugar and served over toast or *flan*
dulce de membrillo, quince preserve
dulce de naranja, marmalade
duquesa, a type of fish or vegetable pie
durazno, peach
eglefino, haddock
ejotes, pole beans
elección, your choice
elotes, corn on the cob

durazno

emborrachada, marinated (means "drunk")
embuchado, stuffed with meat
embutido, fresh sausage
embutido de la tierra, local sausage
empanada (empanadas/os), turnover filled with various ingredients
empanada asturiana, turnover filled with *chorizo*
empanada de gallega, turnover filled with *chorizo*, chicken, ham, peppers and onions
empanada de horno, dough filled with ground meat/ravioli
empanada de lomo, pork and pepper turnover
empanada de pascua, lamb turnover
empanada de vieiras, scallop turnover
empanada salteña, ground meat with pepper, hot sauce, chicken, diced potatoes, olives and raisins wrapped in dough, then baked.
empanada santiaguesa, fish turnover or pie
empanadilla, small fish or meat patty.
    Empanizada means breaded
emparador/emperador, swordfish
emparedado, hot sandwich
empedrada, salt cod and bean salad
encebollada, in an onion sauce/steak smothered in onions
enchilada, cheese-, chicken- or meat-filled *tortilla* topped with sauce.
    Enchiladas and *tacos* are both made of *tortillas* rolled around fillings. The difference is that an *enchilada* is baked with sauce over it and a *taco* is served with the sauce on the side

enchilada roja, sausage-filled *tortilla*

enchilada suiza, stuffed corn *tortilla* topped with *tomatillo* sauce

enchilada verde, meat- or poultry-filled *tortilla* dipped in green tomato sauce

enciam, the Catalan word for lettuce

encurtido, pickle

endibia/endivia, chickory/endive

endrinas, blueberries

enebro, juniper berry

eneldo, dill

encurtido de eneldo.

ensaimada, breakfast sweet roll. A Mallorcan specialty

ensalada, salad/rice salad

ensalada a la almoraina, salad with cumin and tomato dressing

ensalada a la catalana, cod and white-bean salad

ensalada común, green salad

ensalada de frutas, fruit salad

ensalada de habas, cooked bean salad

ensalada del tiempo, seasonal salad

ensalada de pepinos, cucumber salad

ensalada de piparrada, Basque tomato, cucumber and pepper salad

ensalada de pulpo, octopus salad

ensalada de San Isidro, tuna, onion, tomato and lettuce salad

ensalada ilustrada, mixed salad

ensalada koshkera, Basque fish and lobster salad

ensalada mixta, mixed salad

ensalada simple, green salad

ensalada valenciana, salad with lettuce, potatoes and oranges

ensalada verde, green salad

ensaladilla rusa, Russian salad (cold diced potatoes and vegetables with mayonnaise)

entrada, appetizer

entrantes, starters/entrées

entrecot, entrecôt steak/filet mignon

entremés,entremeses, appetizers

entremeses variados, assorted *hors d'oeuvres*

epazote, tea made from an aromatic herb

erizo de mar, sea urchin. In Chile, *erizos* is a dish of raw sea urchins with pepper, salt, oil, onion and parsley. Frequently the sea urchin has a small crab attached to it. Eaten live!

escabeche, pickled/marinated. In Peru, this is a cooked, then chilled fish appetizer served with onions and peppers. In Mexico, this usually is fried fish or shellfish served in a spicy sauce. In the Dominican Republic and Puerto Rico, this refers to frying and then pickling fish, served hot or cold

arengue en escabeche is pickled herring.

escaldums, fried poultry in an onion and tomato sauce

escalfado, poached
escalibada, cod and vegetable salad
escalibada/escalivada, eggplant salad
escaloña, shallot
escalopa, boneless slice of meat
escalope de ternera, veal scallop
escalopines madrileños, veal with tomato sauce
escarcho, red gurnard, a type of fish
escarola, chickory/endive
escocés, scotch
escorpena/escorpión, scorpion
escudella, meat stew
escupinyes, the Catalan word for cockle
espada/espaldilla, swordfish
espadin, sprat/whitebait
espaguetis italiana, spaghetti
espalda, shoulder
esparragados, scrambled eggs and wild asparagus
espárrago, asparagus
espárragos amargueros, wild asparagus
espárragos calientes, asparagus with béchamel sauce
espárragos dos salsas, asparagus with
    mayonnaise and vinaigrette
espárragos trigueros, wild asparagus
especialidad, special
especialidad de la casa, house specialty/chef's specialty
especialidad de la región, regional specialty
especias, spices
espeto, cooked on a spit
espina, fish bone
espinaca, spinach
espinazo, ribs
espuma de chocolate, chocolate mousse
espuma de jamón, ham mousse
espuma de mar, angel food cake with whipped cream.
    A specialty of Uruguay
espumoso, sparkling wine or beverage
esqueixada, red pepper, tomato and cod salad
estacíon, in season
estilo de, in the style of
estofado, stewed/braised.
    Estofados means stews
estofado de vaca, garlic beef stew
estornino, mackerel (chub)
estragón, tarragon

escocés con hielo.

espárrago

espinas

Estofado & Fabada are favorite meals of ours.

faba/fave, a type of bean grown between rows of olive trees in Spain.
Fabes/Faves (the plural of *faba/fave*) are dried for use in
winter and eaten fresh in summer. Large and flat,
they can be brown, beige or green.
Faves are an important part of Spanish
cuisine, especially in Catalonia,
along the Mediterranean

fabada asturiana, pork, beans, sausage and bacon stew. The
traditional version of this dish includes all cuts
of pork, including feet and ears

fabes a la Catalana, stew with beans and black pudding

fabes a la granja, white-bean dish

fabricacion casera, homemade

faisán, pheasant

faisán a las uvas, pheasant and grapes cooked in port

faisán al modo de Alcántara, pheasant with port and truffles

faisán de Alcantara, pheasant in Madeira wine sauce

fajitas, really a "Tex-Mex" dish of grilled strips
of meat or shrimp served on a sizzling
plate and eaten with *tortillas*

falda rellena, stuffed flank

faramallas, sweet fritter

farinato, a sausage made from pork,
flour and lard, generally eaten with fried eggs

farro, vegetable soup with barley

faves, see *faba/fave* above

fesol, dried bean

fetge, the Catalan word for liver

fiambre, any type of cold meat. In Guatemala, meat, fish and
cheese salad

fiambre de bonito, tuna

fiambre de paleta, ham made of shoulder

fideos, noodles

fideua, noodle *paella*/baked noodle dish

figues, the Catalan word for figs

filete, fillet (fish or steak). *Filete migñón* is filet mignon

filete de lenguado, fillet of sole

filete de lomo, tenderloin

filete de res, beef steak

filloas, filled crêpes

fino, pale, dry sherry

flam, the Catalan word for custard

flamenca, a la, with sausage, green peppers, tomatoes, onions and peas

flamenquines, ham and/or cheese rolled into bread and then fried

flan, caramel-custard dessert

flan de café, coffee-flavored caramel custard

flaó/flaón, cheesecake

flauta, filled and deep-fried *tortilla* topped with sauce

flanta means flute.

flor de calabaza, pumpkin flower

flores, flower-shaped fritter

fonda, inn (frequently serving food)

fondo de alcachofas, artichoke heart

formatge, the Catalan word for cheese

forn, al, the Catalan word for baked

frambuesa, raspberry

francesa, a la, in a white sauce/sautéed in butter

fregit, the Catalan word for fried

fresas, strawberries

fresas.

fresas de bosque, wild strawberries

fresco, chilled/fresh. In Central America, this refers to fruit juice

fresón, large strawberry

fricadelas, meat patties

fricandó, fried beef or veal

fricasé, a stewed chicken dish from Puerto Rico and the Dominican Republic (can also contain stewed goat or rabbit)

fricassé, pork cooked in a spicy sauce and served with potatoes and corn. A Bolivian specialty

frijoles, beans (kidney or red beans)

frijoles negros, black beans

frijoles refritos, (refried beans) beans mashed and fried

frío/fría, cold

fritada, fried pieces of meat

fritanga al modo alicante, tuna, fried peppers and garlic

frite, lamb fried with paprika. A specialty in the Spanish region of Extremadura

fritillas, rolls (frequently *fritillas al moro*, pork chunks wrapped in bacon and served on a toothpick)

frito, fried. This can also refer to a dish of fried offal and vegetables

frito de patata, deep-fried potato

fritos con jamón, fried eggs and ham

fritos de la casa, fried appetizers

fritura, fry. *Frituras*, fried bread

fritura (mixta) de pescado, fried mixed fish

frivolidades, assorted pastries

frixuelos, pancakes with honey

fruïta, the Catalan word for fruit

fruta, fruit

fruta de Aragón, chocolate-coated fruit

fruta escarchada, candied fruit (crystallized fruit)

frutas

frutas de mar, seafood

frutillas, strawberries. This word is used in Latin America

fuego de leña, al, charcoal broiled

fuerte, extremely spicy

fuerte can also mean rich. Literally it means strong.

fundido, fondue
gachas, porridge
gachas manchegas, sweet porridge
gallega, a la, with oil and paprika
galletas, crackers/cookies/biscuits/bread rolls
galletas de nata, sandwich cookies
gallina, chicken (hen)
gallina a la cairatraca, chicken stew
gallina de guinea, guinea hen
gallina en pepitoria, chicken stew with
    almonds and/or peppers
gallineta, Norway haddock
gallo, rooster
gallo, flatfish
gallo en chica, rooster in El Salvador
gallo pinto, the national breakfast of Costa Rica.
    Mixed cooked beans and rice.
    Also found in Nicaragua
gallos, *tortilla* filled with meat and sauce
galludo, small shark
galupe, grey mullet
gambas, shrimp/prawns
gambas a la americana, shrimp with garlic and brandy
gambas al ajillo, shrimp sizzled in oil and garlic
gambas a la plancha, grilled shrimp (in the shell)
gambas al pil-pil, shrimp with oil, garlic and hot peppers.
    Served on toothpicks, this is a popular *tapa*
gambas con gardinas, battered, deep-fried shrimp
gambas con mayonesa, shrimp cocktail
gambas en garbardina, shrimp cooked in batter
gambas grandes, prawns
gandinga, spicy kidneys, hearts and livers
gandules, pigeon peas
ganso, goose
garbanzos, chickpeas
garbanzos a la catalana, chickpeas with sausage and tomatoes
garbanzos con espinacas, chickpea, spinach and garlic stew
garbure navarro, pork, vegetable and sausage soup
garobo, iguana
garrapiñadas, glazed
gaseado, glazed
gaseoso, drink with carbonation. This can
    also refer to carbonated lemonade
gâteau basque, filled sweet pastry
gazpacho (andaluz), purée of tomatoes,
    vinegar, onions, green peppers, garlic,
    cucumbers and bread crumbs (chilled)

gallina

gallo.

gallo pinto means painted rooster.

ganso

You can put garobo on the list with curi and cusoco

80

gazpacho blanco, creamy, white *gazpacho* with almonds

gazpacho extremeño, white *gazpacho*

gazpacho malagueño, white *gazpacho* with grapes

gazpacho manchego, pâté of mixed game or stew of game, meat or poultry and vegetables and thickened with unleavened bread

gazpachuelo, soup with potatoes, mayonnaise, fish and vinegar

gelatina, gelatin *jello - you just can't get away from it.*

gelat, sorbet

germen de trigo, ground duram wheat

ginebra, gin

girasol, sunflower *gira sol.*

gitanilla, a la, with garlic

glorias, small sweet pastry

gol, alcoholic beverage from Chile made of milk, butter and sugar

gordal, large green olive

gorditas, small, thick *tortillas* filled with chopped meat, cheese, beans and vegetables, fried, and served with lettuce and chili sauce on top

gordo, fat/fatty *gorditas - deliciosas!!*

gracias, thank you

graella, a la, the Catalan word for grilled

granada, pomegranate

granadina, pomegranate syrup mixed with wine or brandy. This also refers to an eggplant and cured-ham loaf. This can also refer to an almond cookie

grande, large

granizado, fruit sorbet/crushed ice drink with fruit syrup or sweetened coffee

granos de maíz, sweet corn

gran reserva, wine of an exceptional vintage, aged for a long period of time

granvas, sparkling wine

gratén/gratín/gratinado, au gratin *granvas.*

greixera, casserole

greixonera de brossat, cheesecake made from cottage cheese

grelos, turnips/greens

grenadina, grenadine (pomegranate syrup)

grillado, boneless (for example, *pollo grillado* is boneless chicken)

grosella, currant

grosella espinosa, gooseberry

grosella negra, blackberry *grosella negra.*

grosella roja, red currant

guacamole, avocado purée. In Mexico, a dip of mashed avocado, tomato, onion, cilantro and chilies

guanabana, custard apple

guandú, pigeon peas (beans)

guarapo, potent alcoholic beverage made from sugar cane
guarnición, garnish
guasacaca, relish of tomatoes, lime juice, onions and avocado
guayaba, guava. *Pasta de guayaba* is guava paste
guayoyo, large cup of mild, black coffee. Found in Venezuela
guinda, a sour black cherry
guindada, cherry brandy
guindilla, small, hot pepper/hot pepper sauce
guineo, Puerto Rican word for banana
guineitos verdes en escabeche, pickled green plantains.
　　A Puerto Rican dish
guirlache, almond-and-anise candy similar to toffee
guisado, casserole/stew with cooked dish
guisantes, peas
guisantes a la española, peas with cured ham
guisat de cigrons, stewed chickpeas
guiso, stew/soup

guisantes.

guiso de maíz, thick corn stew. A Costa Rican dish
guiso de trigo, turnip soup
gusanos de maguey, fried white grubs. A dish found in parts of Mexico
gusto, a su, your own way
habañero, watch out! The hottest of all peppers
habas, beans. *Habas con jamón* is a casserole of ham and beans
habas a la andaluz, beans with cumin and artichoke
habas a la catalana, faba beans with sausages and meat
habichuela, bean
habichuela (verde), green bean
hallacas, meat and any number of ingredients and spices stuffed in
　　dough then wrapped in banana leaves and boiled in water
hamburguesa, hamburger
harina, flour
harina de maíz, corn meal
hecho, bien, well-done
hecho, muy, well-done
hecho, poco, rare
helado, ice cream

hamburguesa.

helado de mantecado, custard ice cream
helado de nata, custard ice cream
helado de sobores variadas, mixed ice creams
helado quemado, bowl of ice cream topped with grilled sugar
helote, sweet corn-pudding ice cream
hervido, boiled, poached. This can also refer to a Venezuelan soup of
　　vegetables, spices and meat
hielo, ice
hielo, con, a drink "on the rocks"
hierba, herb
hierba buena, mint

hielo.

hierba finas, chopped mixed herbs
hierba luisa, lemon-flavored herbal tea
higadillos, chicken livers
hígado, liver
hígado de ternera, calf's liver
hígado encebollado, liver and onions
higiditos, chicken livers
higo, fig. *Higos secos* are dried figs
higos a la Malagueña, figs, Málaga style.
    A Spanish specialty of sliced figs,

figs - relatively uncommon in most of the United States, are ubiquitous in Spain, South and Central America, eaten raw, dried and prepared.

    wine and sugar
hinojo, fennel
hojaldre, flaky or puff pastry
hojas de laurel, bay leaves
hojas de parra, vine leaves
hojiblanca, black olive
holandas, grape spirit
hongos, mushrooms
horchata, iced, creamy drink made with honey and almonds.
    Sometimes made with tiny crushed artichokes known as tiger nuts.
    In El Salvador, this is a rice-based sweet beverage (usually served
    in a plastic bag). Watch out for the purity of the water. In Costa
    Rica, this is a clear alcoholic beverage made from corn. Be careful,
    this can be dangerous!
horchata de almendra, beverage made of ground almonds
hormiga culona, fried ants! Still found in Colombia
hormigas rojas, red ants (served live) with salt and lime.
    Served in parts of Mexico *gracias, pero NO.*
hornazo, cake (served at Easter)/sausage-stuffed bread
horno, baked/oven
horno, al, baked/roasted
hortaliza, greens
hostería, informal restaurant, usually associated with an inn
huachinango, red snapper. *A la Veracruzana* (Veracruz style) with
    tomato sauce, capers, green olives, onions and yellow peppers
huerta, with assorted vegetables
hueso, bone
hueso de santo, "bone of the saint": *hueso.*
    candied egg yolk in an almond roll. It looks like a bone
huevas, fish roe/fish eggs
huevas prensadas, tuna roe/tuna eggs
huevo hilgado, garnish of shredded boiled eggs
huevos, eggs *huevos*
huevos a la española, eggs stuffed with tomatoes
    and served with a cheese sauce
huevos a la flamenca, eggs baked with tomatoes, vegetables
    and sausage

huevos al la madrileña, baked eggs with sausage and sliced tomato

huevos a la mexicana, scrambled eggs with onions and peppers

huevos al nido, rolls filled with tomato sauce and egg yolk and topped with beaten egg whites, then baked

huevos al plato, fried eggs

huevos al salmorejo, baked eggs with asparagus, pork sausage and ham

huevos cocidos, hard-boiled eggs

huevos con tocino, eggs and bacon

huevos de mújol, Mediterranean caviar (grey-mullet roe)

huevos duros, hard-boiled eggs

huevos duros con mayonesa, hard-boiled eggs with mayonnaise

huevos escalfados, poached eggs

huevos estilo extremeña, vegetables with ham and eggs

huevos flamencos, see *huevos a la flamenca.*
These "Gypsy eggs" are a traditional dish from Seville and the ingredients vary greatly, incorporating whatever is at hand

huevos fritos, fried eggs

huevos motuleños, *tortillas,* fried eggs, black beans, ham and tomato sauce. A Mexican breakfast dish

huevos pasados por agua, soft-boiled eggs

huevos pericos, scrambled eggs

huevos poché, poached eggs

huevos por agua, soft-boiled eggs

huevos rancheros, fried eggs served with a hot tomato sauce; literally, "ranchers' eggs," served to Mexican laborers in the morning.
Today it is served in the morning and as a snack at any time

huevos rellenos, deviled eggs

huevos revueltos, scrambled eggs

huit la coche, mushroom-like corn fungus

humita, In Chile, ground corn wrapped in a corn husk and boiled. Highly seasoned. In Ecuador, this refers to a sweet-corn *tamale*

húngaros, spicy sausage found in Uruguay

infusiones, herbal teas

inglesa, a la, rare meat/served with boiled vegetables

intxaursalsa, A Basque walnut cream

iogur, the Catalan word for yogurt

IVA, (VAT) Value Added Tax. *IVA no incluido* means VAT not included

jabalí, boar

jaiba, Latin American crab

jalapeño, green, very hot pepper. Of the over 60 varieties of chilies found in Mexico, this one is hot, but not murderously so

jalea, jelly

jamón, ham

jamón cocido, boiled ham

jamón de York, cooked ham on the bone

jamón en dulce, ham boiled and served cold

[handwritten margin notes: "huevos frite", "huevos poché", "Don't miss the Museo de Jamó an interesting and popular restaurant chain."]

jamón gallego, smoked ham
jamón ibérico, cured ham
jamón serrano, thin slices of cured ham (like prosciutto)
japuta, pomfret (a deep-water fish). Means "son of a bitch"
jarabe, syrup of fresh fruit
jardinera, a la, served with vegetables
jarra, carafe/pitcher
jarrete, hock/shin bone
jengibre, ginger
jerez, sherry

jerez.

jerez, al, braised in sherry
jerez almontillado, older *jerez fino*.
    Aged at least eight years in wood
    with a gold color and nutty flavor
jerez fino, pale dry sherry
jerez manzanilla, slightly sharper sherry than *jerez fino*
jerez oloroso, dark, full-bodied sherry.
    Most are sweet. The best are dry
jerez palo cortado, a rare sherry, light and gold with a
    complex "character"
jerez seco, dry sherry
jeta, pig's cheek
jibia, cuttlefish
jícama, a root vegetable similar to a potato, usually eaten raw with
    sweet tropical fruit found in Latin America
jitomate, tomato (in Latin America)
jobo, hogplum, a type of plum found in Puerto Rico. The fruit is oval,
    yellow and a couple of inches long, and is usually used to
    make jelly
judías, dried beans
judías blancas, white beans
judías negras, black beans
judías rojas, red beans
judías verdes, green or string beans
judiones, broad beans
judiones de la granja, broad beans with sausage and pig's foot
jueye, land crab (in Puerto Rico)
jugo, juice/fruit juice/gravy
jugo de fruta, fruit juice
jugo de naranja, orange juice
jugo de pomelo, grapefruit juice
jugo de tomate, tomato juice
jugo, en su, in its own juice
juliana, with shredded vegetables
julivert, parsley
jurel, mackerel
kaki, persimmons

*jugo de
naranja
y ron.*

kirsch, cherry liqueur
kokotxas, Basque dish of tender glands near the throat of cod
kuchen, pie (a word used in parts of Latin America)
lacón, ham (boiled)/pork shoulder
lacón curado, salted pork
lamprea, lamprey (seafood)
lamprea de mer, eel
langosta, lobster
langosta a Arragón, lobster in a pepper sauce
langosta a la Catalana, lobster in a ham, mushroom and white sauce
langosta a la Costa Brava, lobster in tomato sauce
langosta a la vasca, lobster in a seafood sauce
langosta con pollo, lobster and chicken in a tomato stew
langostinos, shrimp/prawns
langostinos con clavo, shrimp in a clove-scented marinade
lapa, large roasted rodent! Found in Venezuela *NO, THANKS.*
lardo, lard
laurel, hojas de, bay leaves
lebrada de progonaos, rabbit stew in wine sauce
lebrato, rabbit *lebrato.*
lechal/lechazo, milk-fed lamb
leche, milk
lechecillas de ternera, calf's sweetbreads
leche desnatada, skim milk
leche enter, whole milk
leche frita, creamy custard with a hard crust
leche manchada, milk with a dash of coffee
leche merengada/leche meringuada, cold milk with meringues
      (ice milk)
leche quemada, a Mexican dessert made of vanilla and sugar
lechón, pork
lechona, suckling pig in Latin America
lechón al horno, a Bolivian dish of roast pork with sweet potatoes
lechón asado/lechóna asada, roast suckling pig
lechosa, papaya
lechuga, lettuce
legumbres, vegetables
lengua, tongue
lengua de gato, "cat's tongue": thin, crisp cookies
lenguado, sole
lentejas, lentils *lenguado.*
lentejas onubenses, lentils with spicy sausage and onions
levadura, yeast/baking powder/any leavening agent
levadura quimica, baker's yeast
liadillos, stuffed meat/cabbage rolls
liba, sea bass
licor, liquor

licor de bellota, a liquor made from acorns found in Extremadura
licor de petalos, rose-petal liquor
licuado, milk shake/fruit juices mixed with water
liebre, hare
lima, lime
limón, lemon
limonada, lemonade
lisa, grey mullet. In Venezuela, this can refer to tap beer
liscos, omelette with bacon
lista de platos, menu
lista de precios, list of prices
listo de vinos, wine list
liviano, light beverage
llagosta, lobster dish. Words that begin with *ll* are usually Catalan words
llagosta a la catalona, crayfish with wine and chocolate
llamantol, lobster
llapingacho, mashed potatoes with cheese (with a fried egg on top).
     A specialty in Ecuador
llauna, a la, baked
llegumet, beans, rice and potato dish
llenguado, sole
llet, milk
llimona, lemon
llobarro, bass
lluç, hake
lobarro, bass
locha, loach (carp)/cod
locrio de cerdo, pork and rice dish. A
     specialty in the Dominican Republic
locro, A Latin American corn and meat soup
lombarda, red cabbage
lomo, loin. *Lomito* is tenderloin
lomo a lo pobre, beef topped with two eggs, served with french fries.
     A Chilean dish
lomo bajo, sirloin
lomo curado, cured pork sausage
lomo de cerdo con leche, pork loin pot roast in milk
lomo embuchado, cured smoked pork loin
lomo montado, "mounted steak": tenderloin with two eggs on top and
     served with rice and fried bananas. A Bolivian specialty
lomo relleno, steak stuffed with spices and herbs (especially cilantro).
     A specialty in Panama
lomo saltado, stir-fried steak served with onions, rice, tomatoes and
     vegetables. A Peruvian specialty
lonch, lunch (you will sometimes see this on menus in Mexico)
lonchas de jamón, slices of cured ham
longaniza, long spicy sausage

lonja, thick slice of meat
lubina, sea bass
lubina albufera, sea bass with paprika sauce
lubina a la cantábrica, bass with white wine, lemon and garlic
lubina a la marinera, bass in a parsley sauce
lucia/lucio, pike
macarones/macarrones, macaroni
macarrones gratinados, macaroni and cheese
macedonia de frutas, fruit salad
machacón, boiled potato dish
machas, clams. A word used in Chile
macho, large green banana found in Latin America
madejas, lamb intestines
madrileña, a la, with tomatoes, sausage and paprika/with peppers
madrileño, with lemon and oil
maduixes, the Catalan word for strawberries
maduro, ripe
magdalenas, spongecakes/muffins
magras con tomate, fried ham in a tomato sauce
magro, lean
magro con tomate, fried ham in tomato sauce
mahón, mild cheese
mahonesa, mayonesa, mayonnaise
maíz, corn
majarete, corn meal and custard dessert.
    A specialty in the Dominican Republic
málaga, sweet dessert wine
mallorquina, a la, highly seasoned seafood
malta, malt beverage with barley, sugar cane and hops (non-alcoholic).
    Found in Puerto Rico. In Latin America, dark beer
malteada, milk shake
malvasia, sweet dessert wine
mamey, sweet red/orange tropical fruit
    (mammee apple)
manchego, hard sheep's-milk cheese
mandarina, tangerine
mandioca, cassava, a starchy, boiled root served like mashed potatoes.
    Found on menus in Paraguay
mangetes, the Catalan word for beans
mango, mango. In southern Puerto Rico, the mangos have a flavor
    similar to pineapples
maní (manises), peanut (peanuts)
manitas de cerdo, pig's feet
manitas de cordero, leg of lamb
manjar blanco, a soft toffee dessert found in Colombia and Peru
manojo, bunch/handful
manos de cerdo, pig's feet

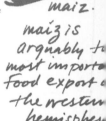
maíz.

*maíz is
arguably t
most importa
food export o
the wester
hemispher*

mamey.

manteca, butter in Argentina and Uruguay

mantecado, vanilla ice cream/small butter cake/creamy cinnamon-flavored custard

mantega, the Catalan word for butter

mantega colorada, spicy pig's fat (usually spread on toast)

mantequilla, butter

manzana, apple

manzana en dulce, apple in honey

manzanas al horno, baked apples

manzanas asadas, baked apples

mantequilla.

manzanilla, herbal tea (camomile tea)

manzanilla, pale dry sherry (slightly sharper than *jerez fino*)

manzanillas, green olives known as Seville olives

margarita.

maracuya, passion fruit

margarina, margarine

margarita, tequila with lime juice

Que bueno!

maria, whiting

mar i muntanya, a dish of shrimp and chicken

marinado, marinated

marinera, a la, This can mean many different things. Usually it means with tomatoes, herbs, onions and wine. Can also mean cooked with seafood in hot sauce

a la marinera means Sailor style.

marisc, the Catalan word for shellfish

mariscada, mixed shellfish/shellfish in a parsley, wine, olive oil and garlic sauce

mariscos, seafood. *Mariscos del día* means fresh seafood

marisquería, seafood restaurant that frequently has tanks of live seafood

mar i terra, chicken and seafood dish

marmitako, Basque tuna stew

marquesa de chocolate, chocolate mousse

marquesita, chocolate confection

marrajo, shark

marrón, a large cup of strong coffee with a small amount of milk (in Venezuela)

marroncito, small cup of strong coffee with a small amount of milk (in Venezuela)

maruca, large cod

más, more

masa, pastry/dough/pasta. In Mexico, the corn dough used to make *tortillas*

matalahuga, matalahuva, anise

matambre, beef roll stuffed with vegetables

maté, caffeinated drink (found in Latin America) similar to tea and made from the leaves of a member of the holly family.

maté. is very bitter.

maté de coca, coca-leaf tea

mat mulo, very fresh

mavi, beer made from tree bark. Found in Puerto Rico

mayonesa, mayonnaise

mazamorra, thick meat and corn soup. A Colombian specialty

mazamorra morada, fruit pudding made from purple corn.
    A Peruvian specialty

mazapán, marzipan

mechada, although this can mean any number of things, it most often
    refers to a roast

medallones, medallions/small steaks/fish steaks

media/medio, half

media botella, half-bottle

medialuna, breakfast croissant found in Argentina

media luna means half moon.

mediana, a large bottle of beer

media noche, small, sweet bun glazed with egg/pork,
    ham and cheese sandwich found in Puerto Rico

mejillones, mussels

mejorana, marjoram

melaza, molasses

marjoram is closely related to oregano.

mel i mató, cream cheese with honey

melindres, marzipan biscuits

melocotón, peach

melón, melon

melón al calisay, melon with liquor poured on top

membrillo, quince

menestra, vegetable soup

menestra de Tudela, asparagus stew

menestra, as in minestrone

menjar blanco, dessert with cream, lemon and ground almonds

menta, mint. *Menta poleo* is mint tea

menú, menu

menú de degustación, taster's menu

menú de la casa, often means fixed-price menu

menú del día, menu of the day

menú fijo, fixed-price menu

menú turístico, tourist menu (usually fixed price)

menudillos, chicken giblets

menudo, offal/tripe (the lining of an animal's stomach)

Some people consider menudo to be a cure for hangovers

menudos gitanos, tripe with ham, garlic, saffron and cumin

merendero, an open-air snack bar

merengada, fruit juice, milk and sugar

merengues, meringues

merienda, snack. In Mexico, this is usually a late-evening snack

merlano, whiting (seafood)

merluza, hake (a fish with white flaky flesh)

merluza a la castellana, hake with shrimp, clams, eggs and chili

merluza a la gallega, hake with potatoes and paprika

merluza a la koskera, a Basque dish of hake with clams

merluza a la madrileña, hake with ham and cheese, rolled in bread crumbs and topped with tomato sauce

merluza a la vasca, hake in a white wine and parsley sauce

merluza en salsa verde, hake in a parsley sauce

mermelada, marmalade/jam

mero, grouper/perch/sea bass

mero a la levantina, grouper with rosemary and lemon juice

mero.

mesa, table

mescal/mezcal, alcoholic beverage made from the agave (maguey) plant (similar to tequila)

mesón, simple, local restaurant

mezclado, mixed

michelada, beer, ice and lime juice

michirones, beans stewed with chili peppers and sausage

miel, honey

mielga, a type of shark

miel y mató, honey over cream cheese

miera cielo, cod and red-pepper salad

migas, croûtons/sautéed breadcrumbs

mielga.

migas canas, bread pudding with milk and breadcrumbs

mijo, millet

milanesa, breaded and fried veal cutlet

milanesa, a la, can mean either breaded and fried or served with cheese

milanesa de carne, sliced beef, breaded and then deep fried. A specialty in Argentina

milanesa de pollo, slices of chicken, breaded and then deep fried. A specialty in Argentina

milanesa res, breaded and fried steak

minuta, menu

minutas, honey-flavored drink made with crushed ice. Found in El Salvador

mistela, wine and grape juice

mixiotes, pieces of chicken served in a spicy sauce

mixto, mixed (can also mean a combination of meats)

mofongo, mashed and then roasted plantain with spices and *chicharrones*. A specialty in the Dominican Republic and Puerto Rico

mogollas, wheat rolls with raisins

mojama, blue-fin tuna

mojara a la plancha, grilled ocean perch

mojarra, bream/fresh water fish/ bluegills

mojete, cod, peppers and onion salad/vegetable dip

mojo, a sauce with spicy peppers

mojo colorado, mixture of paprika, cumin and chili peppers

mojo isleño, Puerto Rican sauce of onions, olives, capers, tomatoes, garlic and vinegar

generally, anything "a la plancha" is grilled.

muy sabroso!

91

mojojones, mussels

mole, thick, dark complex chili sauces invented in Mexico

mole poblano, chicken with sauce of chili pepper, chocolate and spices.
Turkey is substituted for chicken in *mole poblano de guajolote*

mole verde, green sauce with many ingredients including *tomatillos*

moll, red mullet

mollejas, sweetbreads. In Latin America, blood sausage

molusco, snail, mussel or clam (mollusk)

mondongo, seasoned tripe stew

mongetes/monjetes, dried white beans

montado, a type of canapé

montilia, a dry sherry

montilla, dessert wine

mora, blackberry

moraga de sardines, sardine casserole

morcilla, blood sausage/black pudding (made from blood, onions
and rice)

morcilla de ternera, blood sausage made from calves' blood

morcilla dulce, sweet blood sausage. Popular in Uruguay

morcón, a spiced ham

morena, moray eel

moreno, almond meringue

morilla, morel mushroom

morena.

moro, "Moors." In Spain, you will find reference
to *moro* or the Moors who dominated Spain for over 700 years.
This term can mean many things, but frequently means a
spicy sauce

moros y cristianos, black beans and white rice

morragote, grey mullet

morro, cheek

mortadela, salami

morteruelo, mixed-meat hash

moscatel, sweet dessert wine

mosh, oats with honey and cinnamon. A Guatemalan dish

mostachones, "S"-shaped biscuits

mostaza, mustard

mosto, grape juice

*Mosh may sound
exotic but in English
it's mosh. and that
spells Oatmeal in
our book.*

muchacho, beef loin roasted and served in a sauce. A specialty in
Venezuela

mújol, grey mullet

musclos, chicken legs. This is also the Catalan word for mussels

muslo, drumstick of poultry

musola, a type of shark

muy hecho, meat well-done

muy seco, very dry

muzzarella, mozzarella

nabo, turnip

muslo.

nacatamales, *tortilla* filled with meat, corn and sauce and steamed in banana leaves or a corn husk. A Latin American dish

nachos, *tortilla* chips with *frijoles refritos*, grated cheese, *jalapeños*, *guacamole*, black olives and sour cream

ñame, yam in the Dominican Republic

naranja, orange.
Naranja agria (sour orange) is a common seasoning used in Mexico and Puerto Rico

Naranja.

naranjada, orangeade

naranjilla, citrus fruit juice (a cross between peach and orange)

nata, cream

nata batida, whipped cream

natillas, pudding/spiced custard

natural, raw or fresh

navajas, razor clams

navarra, a la, stuffed with ham

navidad, "Christmas": on a menu, this is a dish most likely served at Christmas

nécoras, spider crabs/sea crabs

nectarinas, nectarines

negrito, small cup of strong black coffee (in Venezuela)

Nécoras.

nieves, sorbet (means "snow")

níscalo, wild mushroom

níspero, sapodilla (a rough-skinned, brown fruit from a tropical ever green tree). Found in Puerto Rico

nixtamal, corn-meal dough

nopales, sliced and cooked cactus leaves

nopalito, cactus-leaf salad

ñoquis, the same as the Italian gnocchi (potato dumplings). Popular in Argentina

ñora, mild and sweet peppers

nueces, walnuts

nuez, nut

nuez moscada, nutmeg

ÑORA

oca, goose

ocopa, potatoes or eggs in a spicy sauce. A Peruvian specialty

oil d'oliva, the Catalan word for olive oil

oliaigua, water-based soup flavored with garlic, parsley and olive oil. A specialty in the Balearic Islands

olímpicos, club sandwiches found in Uruguay

olivas, olives

olla, stew. Named after the clay pot it's cooked in

olla de carne, Costa Rican beef stew, usually with plantains and yucca

olla de trigo, chickpea soup with sausage and bacon

olla gitana, thick vegetable stew

olla podrida (putrid pot), stew of meat, poultry, ham and vegetables

olleta, thick, chunky vegetable soup

oloroso, full-bodied sherry. Some are sweet. The best are dry

omelette, omelette. Remember, omelette in Spain is a *tortilla*

once, las, *Once* means eleven – *aguardiente* has eleven letters. So, when someone in Chile says that he is having his "*once,*" it means that he is having a drink of *aguardiente*. *Once* also refers to snacks served in the late afternoon or early evening. Tea or coffee is served with cookies, toast, cheese or other small appetizers

oporto, port

orégano, oregano

oreja (de cerdo), pig's ear

orejones, dried apricots

ortellete, deep-fried pastry flavored with anise

ortiga, nettle

orujo, potent alcoholic beverage made from grapes

If you encounter the letter "O" on a menu it probably means "OR".

oscuro, dark (in color)

ostiones, small local oysters found in Puerto Rico and the Dominican Republic. In South America, this can refer to scallops

ostras, oysters

ous, the Catalan word for egg

Pa amb tomàquet is Catalan for Bread & Tomatoes.

oveja, ewe

pa, the Catalan word for bread

pa amb oli, bread with olive oil and often rubbed with garlic and tomato. A specialty in Mallorca

pa amb tomàquet, toast snack with tomato sauce, olive oil, ham and cheese

pabellón/pabellón criolla, shredded beef in a spicy tomato sauce with rice, plantains and beans. A specialty in Colombia and Venezuela

pacanas, pecans

pachamanca, stew of meat and vegetables cooked in clay pots. A specialty in Peru

pacharán, alcoholic beverage made from the blackthorn fruit (sloe)

pacumutu, In Latin America, beef on a skewer

pa d'ous, flan

paella, saffron-flavored rice with assorted seafood (or with meat). This Spanish specialty is named after the *paellera*, the pan in which *paella* is made

paella

paella a la catalana, *paella* with tomatoes, pork, sausage, squid, red peppers

paella a la marinera, *paella* with seafood

paella a la Valenciana, *paella* with fish and meat (usually assorted shellfish and chicken)

Sin Trabajo means without work

paella al estilo de Parellada/paella sin trabajo, *paella* without shells or bones

paella alicantina, *paella* with fish, onions, green peppers and tomatoes

paella castelana, *paella* with meat

paella huertana de Murcia, assorted-vegetable *paella*

paella marinera, *paella* with fish
paella negra, rice made black by cooking in squid ink
pagre, bream
paico, lemon- and anise-flavored *aguardiente*
paila, fried eggs with bread
pajaritos, small birds
pajuil, cashew
palacones de plátano, fried plantain
palaia petit, sole
paleta/paletillo, shoulder or breast
palitos, skewer
palmeras de hojaldre, puff-pastry dessert
palmitos, hearts of palm
palo cortado, sweet, rare sherry, light and golden with a complex
    "character"
paloma, pigeon
palometa, deep-water fish
palometa blanca, pompano

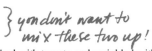

palometa blanca.

palometa negra, pomfret, a deep-water fish
palomitas, popcorn
palta, avocado   *palomitas means little doves.*
palta a la jardinera, avocado stuffed with vegetable salad
palta a rellena, avocado stuffed with chicken salad
pan, bread. ***Barra de pan*** is a loaf of bread
pana, liver
panaché de verduras, vegetable stew with mixed vegetables
pana de coco, coconut bread
pan a la Francesa, french toast
pan aléman, dark bread
panapen, breadfruit
pan blanco, white bread
panceta, bacon/pork belly
pancita, tripe   } *you don't want to mix these two up!*
pancitos, rolls
pan con tomate, bread rubbed with tomato and sprinkled with olive oil
pan de agua, french bread
pan de azúcar, sugar dessert bread
pan de cebada, corn and barley bread
pan de coco, coconut bread
pan de centeno, rye bread
pan de higos, dried fig cake

barra de pan.

pan de horno, baked bread
pan de leche, a cream-topped muffin eaten at breakfast
pan de munición, chocolate-custard cake
pan de pernil, jellied ham
pan de pueblo, long bread loaf
pan dulce, sweet bread

panecicos, fried sweet puff-pastry dessert
panecillos, rolls/small loaves of bread
pan integral, whole-wheat bread
pan negro, dark bread
pan rallado, bread crumbs
panquemado, sugar-glazed bread
panqueques, pancakes

panqueques. Such a cute word, too!

panucho, deep fried *tortilla* filled with refried
beans, meat, tomatoes, sour cream and onions
papa, potato
papas a la criolla, potatoes in a spicy sauce
papas a la huancaína, spicy potato dish with cheese and chili sauce.
A specialty in Peru
papas arrugadas, spicy potato dish
papas bravas, potatoes in cayenne pepper
papas fritas, french fries/potato chips
papas rellenas, stuffed potatoes
papaya, papaya
papazul, *tortilla* filled with diced hard-boiled eggs and covered with a
mild chili sauce popular on Mexico's Yucatán peninsula
parcha, passion fruit
pardet, grey mullet

pardet.

pargo, sea bream/red snapper
parilla, a la, grilled
parilla criolla, marinated beef cooked
on a grill
parillada, mixed charcoal grill of meats, including steak. A word of
advice: in some Latin American countries, this often contains
organ meats not often eaten in the United States and Canada. In
Spain this can refer to a selection of grilled fish
parillada mixta, mixed grill
parrochas, small sardines
pasa de corinto, currant
pasado, done, cooked
pasado bien, well-done
pasado poco, rare

parrochas.

pasas, dried fruit/raisins
pascua, "Easter": on a menu, this is a dish most likely served at Easter
pasta, pasta/soup noodles/can also mean pastry
pastanagues, the Catalan word for carrots
pasta quebrada, a flaky pastry
pastel, pie/cake
pastel de choclo, a corn casserole filled with meats and vegetables.
A specialty in Chile
pastel de higado, liver pâté
pastel de manzana, apple-mint crisp
pastel de pasas, raisin pudding

pastel.

pastelería, pastry shop
pasteles, pastries
pastelillos, small tarts
pastelito, cookies/cupcakes
pastel murciano, veal pie
pastelón de vegetables, vegetable pastry
pastel vasco, filled sweet pastry
pasticho, a dish very similar to lasagna. A specialty in Venezuela
pastilla, bar (as in candy bar) or small candy
pastis, the Catalan word for cake
pastor, al, usually means a pork-based dish
pata, foot
patacó, tuna casserole
patacones, In Ecuador, fried plantains with cheese. In Colombia, mashed potatoes and plantains
patacu, tuna casserole
patas de cordero, stewed leg of lamb
patatas, potatoes
patatas a la leonesa, potatoes with onions
patatas a la pescadora, potatoes with fish
patatas a la riojana, potato and sausage dish
patatas alli olli/patatas alioli, potatoes in garlic mayonnaise
patatas bravas, spicy potatoes with paprika
patatas castellanas, potatoes and paprika
patatas fritas, french fries
patatas nuevas, new potatoes
patatas pobres, potatoes with garlic and parsley
patatas puré, mashed potatoes
patatas viudas, potatoes with fried onions
patatines, diced potatoes
patín, tomato-based sauce
patitos rellenos, stuffed duckling
pato, duck
pato a la naranja/pato a la servillana, duck à l'orange
pavías de pescado, fried fish sticks
pavipollo, large chicken
pavo, turkey
pavo relleno a la catalana, turkey with sausage, plum and pork stuffing
pavo trufado, turkey with truffle stuffing
pay, pie (you'll sometimes find this on menus in Mexico)
pazole, chicken or pork stew with chopped vegetables and herbs
pebre, oil and paprika sauce. Also the Catalan word for pepper
pecho, breast/brisket
pecho de cerdo, pork belly
pecho de ternera, veal breast
pechuga, breast

We've never had tuna casserole anywhere but home, we're wondering if they put potato chips in theirs, too.

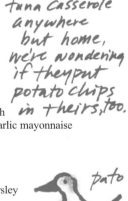

pato.

97

pechuga de pollo, chicken breast

peix, the Catalan word for fish

peix rei, whiting

peixina de pelegri, scallop

pellofa, Balearic Island drink of gin with
   ice, sugar and lemon

pelotas, meatballs

Penedés, a wine-growing region of Spain

pepián, meat stew

pepinillo, pickle

pepino, cucumber

pepitas, sunflower seeds/pumpkin seeds

pepito, sautéed cutlet on a roll

pepitoria, stuffed with tomatoes, green peppers and onions/ fricassee.
   This term has many meanings. For instance, ***pepitoria de pollo***
   is chicken with almonds

pequeño, small

pera, pear. ***Peras al vino*** are pears in a sweet wine sauce

perca, perch

percebes, shellfish/barnacle

perdices (perdíu), partridges (partridge)

perdices a la campesina, partridges with vegetables

perdices a la capellán, ham and pork sausage in a beef roll

perdices a la manchega, partridges cooked in red wine, peppers
   and herbs

perdices a la Torero, partridges with tomato, ham and anchovies

perdigones, partridges

perdiz, partridge

perejil, parsley

perifollo, chervil (an herb)

perilla, a type of bland cheese

pernil, ham/pork shoulder

pernil dolç, the Catalan espression for cooked ham

perrito caliente, hot dog

perruñas/perruñillas, cinnamon cookies

pescadilla, whiting

pescadito, fried fish

pescado, fish

pescados y mariscos, fish and seafood

pèsols, the Catalan word for peas

pestiños, sweet anise-flavored pastries

petit pois, peas (in some parts of Latin America)

peto, white-corn soup with milk. Found in Colombia

pez, fish

pez angel, angelfish shark

pez de San Pedro, John Dory fish (a firm-textured, white-fleshed fish
   with a mild, sweet flavor and low fat content)

98

pez espada, swordfish
pez limón, amberjack
pez martillo, hammerhead shark
pez plata, argentine (a fish similar to salmon)
píbil, dark sauce
picada, thick sauce of garlic, almonds, pine nuts, parsley and saffron
picadilla, creamy almond dressing
picadillo, ground meat/marinated pork and potatoes. In Latin America, this refers to snacks. In Mexico, this is a spicy seasoned ground-meat dish (served as either a main course or as a filling)
picado, ground up
picante, spicy/hot
picante de pollo, fried chicken served with fried potatoes and rice. Very spicy! *Picantes* can also refer to chicken or shrimp served in a spicy red sauce

Picadillo is one of our favorite ~~Foods~~!

picarones/picarrones, deep-fried sweet-potato batter served with syrup. A dish found in Peru
picata, pounded ingredients used to thicken sauces (see *picada*)
picatostes, fried, sugared and buttered toast
pichón, pigeon
pichón con pasas y piñones, pigeon with raisins and pine nuts
pichoncillo, young pigeon, squab
pichuncho, *pisco* and vermouth
pico de gallo, tomato, onion, cilantro and scallion relish (*salsa*)
picoso, hot, spicy
pie (pies), foot (feet)
pierna, leg (of beef)
pijama, caramel custard with ice cream topped with whipped cream
pijotas, baby cod
pijotas, small whiting
pil-pil, al, prepared with oil and garlic
pil-pilando, any dish served sizzling hot
piloncillo, raw sugar
pilongas, dried chestnuts
pilotas, meatballs
pimentón, paprika/cayenne pepper
pimienta de cayena, cayenne pepper
pimienta inglesa/pimienta jamaica, allspice
pimienta/pimienta negra, black pepper
pimiento, bell pepper
pimiento morrón, sweet red bell pepper
pimienton, paprika
pimientos de padrón, fried baby green peppers
pimientos de piquillo rellenos, fried red peppers, stuffed (often with cod)
pimientos fritos, deep-fried green peppers

pimiento.

pimientos rellenos, stuffed peppers
pimientos rojos asados, roasted red-pepper salad
pimientos verde, green peppers
piña, pineapple
piña colada, rum mixed with pineapple juice and cream of coconut
pinchitos, snacks, appetizers/kebabs
pincho moruno, meat kebab. *Pincho de lomito* is tenderloin
    shish kebab
pinchos, snacks served on a toothpick/a dish similar to shish kebab
    This is a specialty in Honduras. This is also the Basque word for
    tapas (pintxos)
pinocillo, alcoholic beverage made from toasted seeds
piñon, pine nut
piñonata, pine-nut cake
pinonos, a mixture of ground beef and plantains dipped in batter
    then fried
pintada, guinea hen
pintarroja, small shark
pintxos, Basque word for *tapas*
piparrada, a Basque word for dishes containing tomatoes and
    green peppers
piparrada vasca, tomato and pepper stew with ham
pipas, seeds
piperita, peppermint
pipián, hot chili sauce. In the Dominican Republic, this is a stew
    containing the intestine of a goat
pipirrana, salad of hard-boiled eggs, tomatoes, peppers, onions, tuna,
    ham, olive oil and garlic
pique a lo macho, chopped beef served with onions and vegetables.
piquete, meat, vegetables and potatoes in a hot-pepper sauce.
piragua, "snow cone" of ice topped with guava or tamarind syrup.
    A Puerto Rican dessert
piriñaca, chopped vegetable salad which often contains tuna
pisco, colorless and potent alcoholic beverage made from corn or grape
    (often mixed with orange juice). This beverage is found in Latin
    America. In Ecuador, it is similar to white rum. *Piscola* is *pisco*
    and coca-cola
pisco sour, lemon juice, sugar and *pisco* shaken together over ice and
    topped with beaten egg whites. A specialty in Ecuador
piso, fried vegetables
pistachio, pistachio nut
pistiñes, sweet anise-flavored fritters
pisto, mixed vegetable, tomato and zucchini salad
pisto manchego, ratatouille/zucchini, tomato and onion stew
pixin, monkfish
plancha (a la plancha)/planchada, grilled
planxa, a la, the Catalan word for grilled

plátanos, bananas. Outside of Spain, this refers to plantains. This
vegetable looks like a banana, but it is picked when green. Unlike
a banana, it is never eaten raw

plátanos flameados, bananas flambéed

plátanos fritos, fried plantains

Platanado is slang for lazy.

plátanos horneados, baked plantains

platija, flounder

plato, dish/plate

plato combinado, combination plate

plato de hoy/plato del día, plate of the day

plato montañero, a Colombian dish with ground beef,
sausage, salt pork, beans, rice, avocado and fried
egg. This dish is also called ***bandeja paisa***

plato típico, any dish which is "typical" to the region or country.
In Nicaragua, a large and inexpensive meal containing any of the
following: beans, rice, meat, fried bananas, *tortillas*, cheese and
a salad

platos combinados, combination plates

plegonero, cod/whiting

poblano, green pepper. Not as hot as a *jalapeño*

poc fet, the Catalan phrase for rare

pochas, beans

pochas a la riojana, black beans in a tomato sauce with sausage
and meat

pocillo, strong black coffee served after dinner in Puerto Rico

poco hecho, rare

poco cocido, rare

poco pasado, rare

poleo, mint

poleomenta, mint tea

pollito, young chicken

pollo, chicken

pollo.

pollo a la chilindrón, sautéed chicken with
tomatoes, peppers and olives

pollo a la mexicana, Mexican-style chicken cooked with onions, green
chili peppers and tomatoes, usually served with rice and beans

pollo al canario, lemon and chicken. A popular dish in the
Canary Islands

pollo al chilindrón, cooked chicken with onions, tomatoes and peppers

pollo asado, roast chicken

pollastre amb gambes, chicken in brandy sauce with shrimp

pollo borracho, fried chicken in a tequila-based sauce

pollo campurriano, rice with bacon,
chicken, shallots and peppers

borracho means drunk.

pollo en arroz, chicken and rice

pollo en cacerola, chicken casserole

pollo en chanfaina, chicken cooked with onions, tomatoes and peppers

pollo en pepitoria, chicken in a wine, garlic and saffron sauce
pollo pibil, chicken simmered in spices. In Mexico, marinated chicken grilled in banana leaves
pollo reina clamart, roasted chicken with vegetables
pollo villeroy, breaded and fried chicken breast in a white sauce
polvorones, hazelnut and/or almond cookies
poma, the Catalan word for apple
pomelo, grapefruit
ponche, punch (usually with brandy)
ponche crema, Venezuelan eggnog
pop, the Catalan word for octopus
porc, the Catalan word for pork

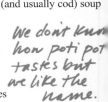

pop.

porcíon, small helping/portion
por favor, please
porotos, kidney beans
porra antequerana, *gazpacho* with ham or tomatoes
porrón, a glass from which you pour wine into your mouth from a distance of at least a foot
porrosaldo/porrusaldo, Basque potato and leek (and usually cod) soup
por unidad, per item
postre de músic, raisin, nut and wine dessert
postres, desserts
potaje, vegetable soup/thick soup (like chowder)
pote asturiana, bean and sausage soup
pote con coles, thick cabbage soup
poti poti, salt-cod salad with peppers and potatoes
pozole, corn and meat stew with hominy
preserva, preserve
préssec, the Catalan word for peach
primer plato, starter/first course
pringadas, fried bread with garlic. After the bread is fried in olive oil and garlic, sausage and ham are served on top. Fattening and delicious!
propina, tip. *No incluyen* (or *incluido*) *propina* means tip not included
provoleta, provolone cheese
pucherete al estilo montañes, spicy blood-sausage stew
puchero, stew. In Uruguay, beef with beans, vegetables, sausage and bacon
puchero bogotana, boiled vegetables, meat and potatoes. A Colombian dish
puchero canario, meat and chickpea casserole. A Canary Islands specialty
pudín, pudding. *Pudín de arroz,* rice pudding
puerco, pork
puerco chuk, pork stew
puerro, leek
pulga, filled roll

We don't know how poti poti tastes but we like the name.

puerro.

102

pulpeta, slice of meat

pulpito, baby octopus

pulpo, octopus

pulpo a fiera a la gallega/pulpo de fiera, octopus with paprika and
   olive oil

pulque, alcoholic beverage distilled from the pulp of the agave
   (maguey) plant. It is much thicker than tequila, which is also from
   the agave plant

punt, a, the Catalan word for medium

punta de diamante, diamond-shaped meringue cake

punta de espárrago, asparagus tip

puntas de filete de res, beef steak (usually sirloin tips) with guacamole
   and beans. A Mexican dish

puntillitas, small squid

punto, a, medium-done

punto, en su, medium-done

punto de nieve, whipped cream with beaten egg whites

pupusa, fried *tortillas* filled with cheese, beans and/or meat. You will
   find *pupusas* and *pupuserías* (snack stands selling *pupusas*) every
   where in El Salvador. In Honduras, *pupusas* are almost always
   filled with pork

puré de patatas/puré de papas, mashed potatoes

purée de apio, celery root which is boiled, puréed and served with salt
   and butter. Some think it tastes like chestnuts

puro de caña, alcoholic beverage made from sugar cane

purrusalda, Basque potato and leek (and usually cod) soup

queimada, apple, brandy, sugar and lemon drink

quemada, topped with caramelized cream

queque, cake

quesada, cheesecake (a dessert made with cheese, honey and butter)

quesadilla, cheescake. In Mexico, grilled or fried *tortilla* filled with
   meat, cheese, potatoes and/or chilies

quesillo, steamed *flan*. This can also refer to cheese

quesillo de leche y piña, milk and pineapple flan found in the
   Dominican Republic

queso, cheese

queso blanco, white cheese

queso de burgos, soft, white, creamy cheese

queso de cabrales, blue cheese (not as strong as Roquefort)

queso de camerano, goat's-milk cheese

queso de Cantabria, mild cheese made from cow's cream

queso de cervera, soft sheep's-milk cheese

queso de hoja, mild soft cheese from Puerto Rico

queso de Idiazábal, strong, creamy, smoky cheese

queso de mahón, semi-hard, tangy cheese

queso de mató, goat's-milk cheese

queso de oveja, mild sheep's-milk cheese

queso de pasiego, fresh soft cheese

queso.

queso de pichón, creamy blue cheese

queso de puzol, fresh cow's-milk cheese

queso de Roncal, strong, creamy sheep's-milk
    cheese (low-fat)

queso de San Simón, strong, smoky cheese

queso de tetilla, pungent, creamy white cheese made
    from cow's milk

queso de Tresviso-Pícon, a blue cheese

queso de villalón, soft cheese made from sheep's milk

queso del país, local cheese

queso fresco, white cheese (similar to feta cheese)

queso fundido, baked cheese dip

queso gallego, a creamy cheese

queso Ibores, goat's-milk cheese with a paprika-coated rind

queso majorero, goat cheese from the Canary Islands

queso manchego, hard, salty, rich and nutty cheese. Spain's best known

queso zamorano, sheep's-milk cheese similar to *queso manchego*

quilet, bream

quinto, a small bottle of beer

quisquilla, shrimp

raba, breaded, fried squid

rábano, radish. *Rabanitos* are small radishes found in Latin America

rábano picante, horseradish

rabo, tail

rabo de buey/rabo de toro, oxtail

racimo, bunch (as in a bunch of grapes)

raciónes, large portion (usually of snacks)

ración piqueña on a menu means small portion.

raf, a type of tomato

ragout, ragoût

raïm, the Catalan word for grape

raíz, root

rajas, slices. In some parts of Latin America, grilled green peppers

rallado, grated

rama, dried hot chili peppers

ramillo, spicy

rana, ancas de, frog legs

rancho canario, stew of sausage, bacon,
    beans, potatoes and pasta. A specialty in the Canary Islands

rap/rape, monkfish/angler fish

raspas de anchoas, deep-fried backbones of anchovies

ravioles, ravioli

raya, ray, skate (seafood)

rebanada, slice

rebozado, coated with breadcrumbs and fried

I'll pass.

recargo, extra charge

redondo, filet of beef

refrescos, soft drink/cool drink. In Costa Rica, fruit shakes. In Puerto Rico, you will find *refrescos del país* signs everywhere. These "drink stands" are often automobile trunks filled with various fruit juices, especially *cocos fríos* (cold drinking coconuts)

refrito, refried

refritos, refried beans

regular, meat done medium

rehogado, sautéed

rellenas/os, stuffed/filled

rellenos de papa, meat-stuffed potatoes fried in batter

remanat d'ous, the Catalan phrase for scrambled eggs

rémol, brill/flounder

remolachas, beets

reo, sea trout

repollo, cabbage

remolachas.

repostería de la casa, house-specialty desserts

requemado, cold rice pudding with sugar topping

requesón, cottage cheese

res, beef

reserva, mature wine (of older vintage)

reserva especial, wine of an exceptional vintage. A step above *gran reserva*

revoltillo, scrambled eggs

revueltos, scrambled eggs

revuelto mixto, scrambled eggs with vegetables

Ribera del Duero, a wine-growing region of Spain

riñón, kidney

riñonada, roasted kidneys

riñones al jerez, kidneys cooked in sherry

rioja, a red wine similar to Bordeaux. Rioja is a wine-growing region of Spain

rioja, a la (a la riojana), served with red peppers

róbalo, haddock/snook

robioles, custard-filled pastry

rocoto, a hot red pepper

rodaballo, turbot/flounder

rollitos, small filled rolls

Róbalo

rollo de carne, meat loaf

rollo de merluza, hake roll in a parsley sauce

romana, a la, dipped in batter and then fried

romero, rosemary

romesco/romescu, mild, sweet chili pepper. This can also refer to a sauce of peppers, tomatoes, ground almonds and hazelnuts

romesco de pescado, mixed fish. *Romesco de peix* is a fish stew popular in the Catalonia region of Spain

ron, rum

ronyon, the Catalan word for kidney

ropa vieja, left-over meat and vegetables cooked with tomatoes and green peppers. In Panama, rice covered with spicy shredded beef and green peppers

ropa vieja means old clothes

rosada, shark

rosado, rosé wine

rosbif, roast beef

rosca/rosco, doughnut

roscon, roll filled with guava jelly and coated with sugar

roscon de reyes, sweetened bread, coated with sugar and candied fruits. A holiday bread with a "charm" hidden inside

rosé, rosé wine

rosquilla, doughnut (usually glazed)

rossejat, cooked rice dish

rostit, the Catalan word for roasted

rovellon, wild mushroom

rubio, red mullet

ruibarbo, rhubarb

Sabores or Sabroso means Savory or tasty.

ruso, cake with custard filling

sábalo, shad (seafood)

sacarina, saccharin

sacromonte, omelette made of eggs, vegetables, brains and bull's testicles. A specialty of Granada

saice, a spicy meat broth

sajta, chicken served in *aji* (hot pepper) sauce. A Bolivian specialty

sal, salt

saladitos, appetizers

salado, salted

salazón, cured (salted fish or meat)

salchicha, pork sausage

salchichas blancas, pork sausage with fried onions

salchichas de Frankfurt, hot dogs, frankfurters

salchichón, salami (cured sausage)

salema, bream

salmó, the Catalan word for salmon

salmón, salmon

salmón ahumado, smoked salmon

Salmón.

salmón a la ribereña, fried salmon steaks

salmonete, red mullet

salmonete en papillote, red mullet cooked in foil

salmorejo, thick sauce of bread, tomatoes, vinegar, green peppers, olive oil and garlic. A variation of *gazpacho*

salmorejo cordobes, chilled *gazpacho*

salmorreta, a smoky tomato sauce

salmuera, in brine

salon de té, tea room

salones, cured lamb or beef

salpicón de mariscos, mixed shellfish salad

salsa, sauce. In Mexico, relish of chopped tomatoes, onions, cilantro and scallions; also called *pico de gallo, salsa crud,* or *salsa fresca*

salsa bechamel, white sauce/béchamel sauce

salsa criolla, spicy sauce used on steaks in Uruguay

salsa de tomate, ketchup/tomato sauce

salsa española, sauce with wine, spices and herbs

salsa hollandaise, hollandaise sauce

salsa ingles, Worcestershire sauce

salsa mayordoma, butter and parsley sauce

salsa picante, hot-pepper sauce

salsa ranchero, red chili sauce with a tomato base

salsa romesco, sauce with tomatoes and garlic or ground nuts and sweet peppers

salsa tártara, tartar sauce

salsa verde, parsley sauce. In Mexico, chilies, cilantro, garlic and green tomato sauce. In Latin America, hot sauce with tomatoes and peppers

salsifí, salsify

salteado/a, sautéed

salteño, turnover filled with meat and sauce

salvado, bran

salvia, sage

sama de pluma, bream

samfaina, sauce of eggplant, zucchini, peppers, onions and tomatoes

sancochado, meat and vegetable stew with spices

sancocho, vegetable soup with meat or fish. In the Canary Islands this is white fish and boiled potatoes

sancocho canario, fish stew with potatoes in a red-pepper sauce

sandía, watermelon

sandwich, sandwich

sandwich caliente, hot sandwich.
In Uruguay, a grilled ham and cheese sandwich

sandwich mixto, often refers to a ham and cheese sandwich

sangre, blood

sangría, chilled red wine, fruit juice, brandy and soda. There are many variations. For example, in Ecuador, red wine, sugar, fruit and lemon juice

sangrita, tequila with lime, orange and tomato juice

santiaguiño, (clawless) lobster

sard, bream

sardinas, sardines

sargo, bream

sarsuela, fish stew (see also *zarzuela*)

sarten, en, from the frying pan

schop, In Chile, beer (usually draft beer)

sebo, fat

seco, dry. Can also refer to dry wine

seco de, stew

seco de cordero, lamb stew

seco de gallina, chicken stew

segundo plato, second course

semi-dulce, semi-sweet

semifríos, molded frozen dessert

semillas, seeds

sémola/semolina, ground duram wheat

sencillo, plain

sepia, cuttlefish

sequillos, hazelnut meringues

serenata, fish in vinaigrette with onions, avocados and vegetables.
    A specialty in Puerto Rico

serrano, thin slices of cured ham (like prosciutto). This also refers to a
    small green chili pepper that is hotter than a *jalapeño*

servicio, service

servicio incluido, service included (tip included)

servicio no incluido, service not included (tip not included)

servilleta, napkin

sesamo, sesami. Can also refer to perch

sesos, brains   *No me gusta!*

seta, mushroom

setas a la bordalesa, mushrooms cooked in red wine and onions

setas salteadas, mushrooms with sausage and garlic

seviche, cold whitefish salad popular in Acapulco, Mexico. *See ceviche*

sevillana, a la, cooked in wine with olives

shangurro, stuffed crab

sidra, alcoholic cider

sidrería, cider house.
    The production of alcoholic cider (*sidra*) takes place mostly in
    the north: Asturias, Galicia and Basque country

sípia, the Catalan word for cuttlefish

sifón, soda water

silpancho, beef (thinly sliced, breaded and fried) served with an egg
    on top

sin, without

sincronizadas, flour tortilla (folded and browned) with ham and cheese

singani, Bolivian alcoholic beverage made from grapes

sin gas, without carbonation

sin trabajo, seafood served with the shells removed (means "no work")

sobrasada, soft *chorizo* (sausage) often used as a spread

sobrebarriga, breaded and stuffed steak

soda blanca, soda water

sofregit, sauteed onions and tomatoes

sofreído, sauteed

sofrito, onions fried with garlic/sautéed. In Puerto Rico, sauté of
    tomatoes, onions, red and green peppers, spices, garlic and
    108 cilantro. Commonly found in stews and bean dishes

soja, soy
soldaditos, fried fish sticks
soldaditos de pavia, fried strips of salt cod
soldat, sole
solla, plaice
solo, neat (straight-up) alcoholic beverage
solomillo, fillet steak/tenderloin/sirloin
solomillo andaluz, pork tenderloin
sol y sombra, brandy and anise-flavored
    liquor (means "sun and shade")
sooyosopy, Paraguayan soup of cornmeal and
    ground meat, usually served with rice

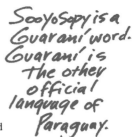

Sooyosopy is a Guaraní word. Guaraní is the other official language of Paraguay.

sopa, soup
sopa a la criolla, spicy noodle and beef soup. A Peruvian specialty
sopa al cuarto de hora, clam, ham, shrimp and rice soup. The
    ingredients vary greatly as it is a soup you can make with whatever
    you have on hand "in a quarter of an hour"
sopa al estilo Mallorca, cabbage soup
sopa alpurrañas, egg and ham soup
sopa cachorreñas, fish soup with orange zest, vinegar and oil
sopa castellana, vegetable soup/garlic soup with cumin. A specialty in
    the Spanish region of Castile-Leon
sopa clara, consommé
sopa criolla dominicana, a soup of stewed meat, greens, onions, spices
    and pasta. A specialty in the Dominican Republic
sopa de ajo, garlic soup *ajo .*
sopa de ajo blanco, cold soup of garlic, grapes and ground almonds
sopa de alubrias negras, thick black-bean soup
sopa de albóndigas, chicken broth with meatballs
sopa de almendras, almond pudding
sopa de aragonesa, soup of calf's liver and cheese, topped with bread
    or cheese crust
sopa de calabaza, squash soup
sopa de calducho, clear soup *calabaza*
sopa de cangrejos, crab bisque
sopa de cebolla, onion soup
sopa de cocido, meat soup
sopa de cola de buey, oxtail soup
sopa de dátiles, brown-mussel soup
sopa de fideos, noodle soup
sopa de frutas de mar, shellfish soup
sopa de galets, pasta and meatball soup
sopa de gallina, chicken soup
sopa de gato, garlic soup with grated cheese
sopa de guisantes, pea soup
sopa de habichuelas negras, black-bean soup
sopa de la cena, pork-sparerib soup

cangrejos .

sopa de lentejas, lentil soup

sopa de lima, chicken and lime soup

sopa de maní, roasted-peanut soup

sopa de mariscos, shellfish soup. In Mexico, tomato and
    seafood chowder

sopa de mejillones, mussel soup

sopa de mondongo, tripe stew or soup

sopa de pasta, noodle/pasta soup

sopa de pescado, fish soup

sopa de picadillo, egg and ham soup

sopa de servillana, spicy fish soup flavored with mayonnaise

sopa de tomate, tomato soup

sopa de tortilla, Mexican soup of
    fried *tortilla* strips, chicken and chilies

sopa de tortuga, turtle soup

sopa de verduras, vegetable soup

sopa de vino, soup containing sherry

sopa del quarto de hora, soup with a base
    of fried onions and rice

sopa espesa, thick soup

sopa liquida, "wet soup" or what we think of as soup. See *sopa seca*

sopa mahimones, soup with olive oil, bread and garlic base

sopa maimones, soup with olive oil, bread and garlic base

sopa mallorquina, thick soup of tomatoes, meat, eggs, onions
    and peppers

sopa mondongo, tripe stew

sopa paraguaya, "Paraguayan soup" of mashed corn bread, cheese,
    onion, milk and eggs

sopa seca, rice or pasta covered with a sauce and served after soup in
    Mexico (means "dry soup"). The second course of a full meal

sopa servillana, spicy fish and mayonnaise soup

sopaipillas, fried pumpkin

sopapilla, deep-fried pastry

sope, Mexican dish of *tortillas* sealed together and filled with meat or
    cheese and fried

sorbete, sorbet/cold fruit drink. In Central America, this can refer
    to ice cream

sospiros de Moros, dry meringues

suave, soft

suc, the Catalan word for juice

sucre, the Catalan word for sugar

suero, whey

suflé, soufflé

sugerencias del chef, chef's recommendations

suizos, breakfast rolls baked with sugar

supremas de rodaballo, thin slices of fish

suquet, fish stew

surrullitos, deep-fried corn sticks stuffed with cheese
surtido, assorted
surubí, a fresh-water fish similar to catfish found in Paraguay
suspiros, dry meringues. In Peru, sweet
    meringue dessert filled with cream
    and often with fudge
suspiros de monja, soft meringue with custard
susquet, assorted fish and shellfish stew
susquillo de pescador, assorted fish and shellfish stew
taberna, tavern
table, a platter of cheese or meat
taco, meat-filled *tortilla* with tomatoes, onions, and other ingredients.
    Dorado means a fried ("U"-shaped, crisp) *taco,*
    and *suave* means plain (not fried)
tajada, slice. In Latin America, fried banana slices
tajaditas, fried banana chips
tallarines, noodles
tallarines a la italiana, tagliatelle
tamale, corn-meal dough filled with meat and sauce and steamed while
    wrapped in banana leaves or a corn husk. In Costa Rica, olives,
    rice and raisins are often included
tamarindo, tamarind
tapa, snack/appetizer.
    Tapa is the Spanish word for lid or cover.
    The bartender will place an appetizer on
    top of your glass of wine or beer
tapado, stew
taronja, the Catalan word for orange
tarragón, tarragon
tarrina, en, served in an earthenware pot
tarta, the Catalan word for tart
tarta alaska, baked Alaska
tarta al whisky, whisky and ice-cream cake
tarta de almendra, almond cake
tarta de arroz, cake containing rice
tarta de manzana, apple tart
tarta de naranja, orange-almond cake
tarta de piñones, pine-nut cake
tarta de Santiago, almond cake
tarta helada, layered ice-cream cake
tartaletas, tartlets. ***Tartaleta de txangurro*** is Basque spider-crab spread
tarta moca, mocha cake
tarta Pasiega, anise-flavored cheesecake
tartar crudo, steak tartare
tasca, a bar serving *tapas*
taza, cup
té, tea

Sospiro means Sigh - Sospiros de Moros means Moor's sighs -

un taco.

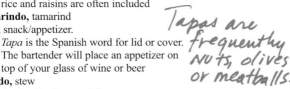

Tapas are frequently Nuts, olives or meatballs.

Albondigas. (meatballs.)

una taza de té.

tecla de yema, candied egg-yolk pastries

té con leche, tea with milk

té con limón, tea with lemon

té helado, iced tea

tejas, egg-white, almond and sugar biscuits

tejos de queso, cheese pastries

tembleque, coconut pudding

tenca, tench (a Eurasian fish)

tenedor, fork

Although a Eurasian fish, tench has been introduced to North America and Australia

tepezcuintle, a Mayan specialty, the largest member of the rodent family

tepín, small, very hot chili pepper

tequeños, fried appetizer of dough
    wrapped around white cheese

tequila, ever had a *tequila* hangover? An alcoholic beverage distilled
    from the pulp of the agave (maguey) plant. Mexican *tequila* is
    often higher proof than *tequila* sold in the United States and
    Canada.

    Four types are: **anejo** (aged in oak barrels for at least
      one year), **gold** or **joven abocado** (unaged
      with color and flavor added), **plata** or **blanco**
      (unaged and sold within two months of distilling)
      and **reposado** (aged from two months to
      one year, means "rested")

tercio, large bottle of beer

tereré, *maté* made with cold water

término medio, medium

ternasco, baby lamb

ternasco asado, lamb roasted in wine and lemons

Tequila.

ternera, veal

ternera a la estremeña, veal cooked in a sauce of onions, *chorizo* and
    sweet peppers

ternera a la sevillana, sautéed veal with sherry and green olives

terrina, pâté

tetería, tea shop

tetilla, a mild, creamy cheese

tiempo, al, at room temperature (***del tiempo*** means "of the season")

tigres, mussels in cayenne-pepper sauce

tila, lime-flavored tea

tinto, black coffee in Colombia

tinto de verano, "summer red," red wine
    with lemon-lime soda water

VINO TINTO

tinto, vino, red wine

tío pepe, a type of sherry

tioro, Basque fish soup

típico de la región, regional specialty

tiradito, fish, lime juice and oil served with pepper sauce.

tisanas, herbal teas

112

tocinillo de cielo/tocino de cielo, very rich crème caramel

tocino, bacon

tocino de cielo, lemon-
or cinnamon-flavored baked custard

tocinillo de cielo was created in the 1600's by Spanish Nuns.

todo incluido, all inclusive (price and service)

tojunto, rabbit, meat and vegetable stew

tomaquets, the Catalan word for tomatoes

tomate, tomato

tomates rellenos, stuffed tomatoes

tomatillo, mild green fruit (similar to a green tomato)

tombet, vegetable stew

tomillo, thyme

tónic/tónica, tonic

tonyina, the Catalan word for tuna

tordo, thrush

toro, bull

toro!

toronja, grapefruit

torrada, the Catalan word for toast

torrados, toasted chickpeas

torreja/torrija, French toast/bread dipped in milk, fried and
sugar coated

torta, cake/breakfast roll topped with sugar. In Costa Rica, meat and/or
cheese sandwich. In Mexico, a sandwich

torta de aceite, plain, bland biscuit

torta de cielo, almond spongecake ("cake of heaven")

torta de hojaldre, puff pastry with jam

torta del casar, soft and creamy sheep's-milk cheese found
in Extremadura

torta de plátano, plantain and cheese cake

torta de Santiago, almond cake

torta milanesa, deep-fried meat sandwich

torta real, "royal cake" with eggs, almonds and cinnamon

tortell, breakfast roll with crushed almonds and lemon filling

tortilla, In Spain, an omelette. In Mexico, a flat, round, cooked
unleavened bread. Corn *tortillas* are the daily starch of Mexico,
made of *masa* (corn flour). In Northern Mexico, *tortillas* are often
made with flour

tortilla a la catalana, omelette with sausage and beans

tortilla a la flamenca, Spanish omelette (see *huevos a la flamenca*)

tortilla a la jardinera, omelette with mixed vegetables

tortilla a la paisana, omelette with mixed vegetables

tortilla aliada, omelette with mixed vegetables

tortilla asturiana, tuna, onion and tomato omelette

tortilla a su gusto, omelette made with whatever ingredients you want

tortilla con quesillo, fried corn *tortilla* with melted cheese

tortilla de escabeche, omelette containing fish

tortilla de harina, flour *tortilla*

tortilla de huevos, omelette

tortilla de jámon, an omelette with ham

tortilla de patatas, potato omelette

tortilla española, omelette with potato and onion filling

tortilla francesa, plain omelette

tortilla gallega, omelette with sausage and peppers

tortilla granadina, omelette with brains, asparagus, peppers and artichokes

tortilla guisada, omelette with tomato sauce

tortilla hormigos, omelette with fried bread crumbs

tortilla murciana, omelette with tomato and red peppers

tortilla paisana, omelette with sausage, potatoes, peppers and tomatoes

tortilla piperrada, red pepper, onion and tomato omelette

tortilla sacromonte, omelette made of eggs, vegetables, brains and bull's testicles. A specialty of Granada

gross.

tortillitas, pancakes

tortita, waffle

tortuga, turtle

tosta, toast with topping

tostada, In Spain, toast. In Mexico, a fried *tortilla* topped with ingredients such as chicken, beans and/or cheese. In Venezuela, a sandwich with crisp bread, meat, cheese or chicken

tostadas de maíz, corn pancakes

tostaditas, Mexican *tortilla* chips. They can also refer to small *tostadas*

tostado, toasted. *Pan tostado* is toast

tostón, suckling pig

tostones, fried plantains

totopos, Mexican *tortilla* chips

tournedó, filet steak

toyina, salted tuna

trasero, rump

trigo, wheat

trucha.

triguillo, turnip soup

tripas, tripe

trozo, rack (as in rack of lamb)

trucha, trout

trucha a la montañesa, trout cooked with white wine and bay leaves

trucha a la Navarra, trout baked with red wine and herbs and often wrapped in bacon

trucha frita a la asturiana, trout floured and fried in butter

trucha molinera, trout floured and fried with butter and lemon

trufa, truffle. *Trufado* means with truffles

truita, omelette. Can also mean trout

trumfes, potatoes

ttoro, Basque fish soup

tubo, a large glass of beer

tuétano, bone marrow

tumbet, vegetable casserole featuring eggplant
tuna, prickly pear
tuntas, freeze-dried potatoes
turrón, nougat. ***Turrón de guirlache*** is almond brittle
txacoli/txakolí, Basque sparkling white wine
txangurro, Basque dish of seasoned crabmeat
ulloa, a soft cheese similar to camembert
unidad, por, per item
urta, sea bream
urta a la roteña, baked bream in an
    onion, tomato and brandy sauce
utensilio, utensil
uvas, grapes
uvas pasas, raisins
vaca (carne de), beef
vaca salada, corned beef
vaina, a sweet sherry-based drink found in Chile
vainilla, vanilla
vainitas, Latin American word for green beans
valenciana, a la, usually means with tomatoes, rice and garlic
vapor, steamed
variada, bream
variado, assorted
vasca, a la, usually means in a garlic, parsley and white-wine sauce
vaso, glass/tumbler
vedella, the Catalan word for veal
vegetales, vegetables
vegeteriano, vegetarian. In some parts of Latin America, ***"no tiene
    carne"*** (literally "does not contain meat") means does not have
    beef, but may contain other meat
venado, venison
veneras, scallops
venta, country inn serving food
veracruzana, a la, (Veracruz, Mexico style) with tomato sauce, capers,
    green olives, onions and yellow peppers
verat, mackerel
verde, green/a common, green, medium-hot pepper
verduras, green vegetables
vermut (vermú), vermouth (white wine blended with herbs and fruit
    peels and fortified with brandy)
vi, the Catalan word for wine
vi blanc, the Catalan word for white wine
vi negre, the Catalan word for red wine
vi novell, new wine similar to Beaujolais Nouveau
vi rosat, the Catalan word for rosé wine
vieira, scallop
villeroy, chicken breasts or prawns coated in béchamel

an X in a word is a sure sign that the word has Basque origins.

uvas.

vi novel.

vinagre, vinegar
vinagreta, vinaigrette
vino, wine
vino añejo, mature wine
vino blanco, white wine
vino clarete, rosé wine
vino común, table wine
vino de aguja, slightly sparkling white or rosé wine
vino de jerez, sherry
vino de la casa, house wine
vino de la tierra, local wine
vino del país, local wine (wine from the country)
vino de mesa, table wine
vino de Oporto, port
vino de pasto, table wine
vino dulce, dessert wine
vino espumoso, sparkling wine
vino generoso, fortified wine
vino rancio, dessert wine
vino rosado, rosé wine
vino seco, dry wine
vino suave, sweet wine
vino tinto, al, baked in a red-wine sauce
vino tinto, red wine
vino verde, white wine from Galicia
viski, whiskey
viudo de pescado, fish stew
vizcaína, a la, sauce of peppers, onions, paprika, and garlic
vodka, vodka
vuelvealavida, seafood cocktail found in Latin America
whisky, whiskey
whisky americano, bourbon
xai, the Catalan word for lamb
xampañ, sparkling wine
xampanyerie, bar found in and around Barcelona serving *cava*
   (sparkling wine)
xampinyons, the Catalan word for mushrooms
xató, salad mixed with tomato, olives,
   anchovies and cod or tuna
xatonada, salad mixed with tomato,
   olives, anchovies and cod or tuna
xerex, another word for *jerez* (sherry)
xocolata, the Catalan word for chocolate
xoric amb patates, swallow with potatoes
xuxos, custard-filled doughnuts
yaguarlocro, potato soup with black pudding (blood sausage).
   A specialty in Ecuador

VINO TINTO. VINO BLANCO.

VINO de Oporto.

in case you couldn't figure this out for yourself.

Xampañ.

yema, egg yoke. This also refers to a small, sweet, yellow cake which looks like an egg yoke

yema de coco, coconut candy

yema (del huevo), yoke of an egg

yerba maté, herbal tea

yogur, yogurt

yogur desnatado, low-fat yogurt

herbal tea is also called tisane.

yuca, sweet potato/cassava (an edible root that yields a starch)

zamorana, a la, with pork cheek and pig's feet

zanahorias, carrots

zanca, shank

zapallo, squash

zapote, sweet pumpkin

zarajo, tripe on a stick

zarangollo, white fish with tomato and saffron/zucchini and onion casserole

zarzamora, blackberry

zarzuela, assorted seafood stew (highly seasoned)

zarzuela de mariscos, highly seasoned shellfish stew

zarzuela de pescados, highly seasoned seafood stew

zarzuela de verduras, vegetable stew

zoque, cold tomato and pepper soup

zorza, pork fried with paprika

zumo, juice. *Zumo de fruta* **is** fruit juice

zumo de fruta fresca, fresh fruit juice

zumo de naranja, orange juice

zumo de naranja natural, freshly squeezed orange juice

zurracapote, hot red-wine punch with brandy and cinnamon/stewed figs and apricots

zurro, white-wine cooler

zurrón, stuffed

Buen Provecho!

Places to Eat

Phone numbers, days closed and hours of operation often change, so it's advisable to check ahead. Restaurants in tourist areas may have different hours and days of operation during low season. Reservations are recommended for all restaurants unless noted. Telephone country codes: Spain is 34 and Portugal is 35.

Prices are for main courses. Lunch, even at the most expensive restaurants listed below, always has a lower fixed price. Credit cards are accepted unless noted otherwise. We have listed the nearest metro stops in Barcelona and Madrid.

Inexpensive: under 10 euros €
Moderate: 11 – 20 euros €€
Expensive: over 20 euros €€€

Barcelona

Abac €€€

Elegant, modern restaurant with a reputation for innovative cuisine. Lovely patio. *Info*: 1 Ave. Tibidabo. Tel. 933196600. Reservations required. Metro: Vallcarca. www.abacbarcelona.com.

Casa Calvet €€€

Splurge at this beautiful restaurant serving Mediterranean cuisine fine enough to match its surroundings. It's known for its extensive wine list. Thanks to famous architect Antoni Gaudí, you'll be dining in a building with extraordinary décor. Gaudí was a religious man. He incorporated much religious symbolism into his architecture. Seek out the large door knockers with crucifixes on them. Underneath each is a smashed bug, a symbol of evil. *Info*: 48 Carrer de Casp.Tel. 934124012. Closed Sun.Metro: Urquinaona. www.casacalvet.es.

Cinc Sentits €€€

The austere modern interior is in great contrast to the lush food served here (the name means "five senses"). *Info*: 58 Carrer d'Aribau (at Carrer d'Aragó). Tel. 933239490. Closed Sun and Mon. Metro: Passeig de Gràcia. www.cincsentits.com.

Botafumeiro €€-€€€

Large and bustling (can you say "noisy"?) restaurant known for its seafood dishes (don't worry, they have meat dishes also). Waiters dressed in white jackets will serve you very good food (try the *paella*). It's worth the trip. *Info*: 81 Gran de Gràcia. Tel. 932184230. Closed part of Aug. Metro: Fontana. www.botafumiero.es.

Osmosis €€-€€€

This small restaurant with a fixed menu gets rave reviews. You'll dine on traditional Catalan cuisine, and they'll accommodate you if you're a vegetarian. Hospitable staff. *Info*: 100 Aribau. Tel. 934545201. Closed Sun and Mon. Metro: Provença. www.restauranteosmosis.com

Café de L'Acadèmia €€
On the Plaça Sant Just in the Gothic Quarter, offering Catalan specialties (especially roasted meat dishes) at reasonable prices. The interior has old stone walls, and you can even dine in the wine cellar. In good weather, you can sit on the terrace with views of the oldest fountain in Barcelona. Good pasta dishes. *Info*: 1 Carrer Lledó. Tel. 933198253. Closed weekends and part of Aug. Metro: Jaume I.

Cal Pep €€
Catalan food, especially seafood, at this bustling restaurant not too far from the church Santa Maria del Mar. There are only five tables in the back, but the action is at the bar. *Info*: 8 Plaça de les Olles. Tel. 933107961. Closed Sun, Mon (lunch), Sat (dinner), and Aug. Metro: Barceloneta. www.calpep.com.

Can Majó €€
Near the beach in La Barceloneta, known for its fresh seafood dishes and *paella*. *Info*: 23 Carrer Almirall Aixada. Tel. 932215455. Closed Sun (dinner) and Mon. Metro: Barceloneta. www.canmajo.es.

Els Quatre Gats €€
"The Four Cats," in operation since the late 1800s, serves simple Catalan cuisine. The café is absolutely stunning. Picasso used to hang out here. *Info*: 3 Carrer Montsió. Tel. 933024140. Open daily. Metro: Plaça de Catalunya. www.4gats.com.

La Crema Canela €€
Just off the Plaça Reial, this attractive, small restaurant serves modern Mediterranean and Asian fare. *Info*: 6 Passeig Madoz (off of Plaça Reial). Tel. 933182744. Open daily. Metro: Jaume I. www.lacremacanela.com.

Taxidermista €-€€
Right on the lovely Plaça Reial, this popular eatery has good food and is known for its serious people-watching. It was here (when this space housed a taxidermy shop) that Salvador Dalí purchased a stuffed elephant and had his photo taken on it in the square. Try the *pa amb tomàquet* (a local snack with tomato sauce and olive oil). *Info*: 8 Plaça Reial. Tel. 934124536. Closed Mon and part of Jan. Metro: Liceu. www.xidermista.com.

Casa Alfonso €-€€
This *tapas* bar is decorated with murals of the city in the early
20th century. Try the cheese platter served on a wooden plank.
Info: 6 Carrer de Roger de Llúria. Tel. 933019783. Closed Sun.
Metro: Urquinaona. www.casaalfonso.com.

Bar Mut €-€€
Intimate, friendly and popular wine and *tapas* bar.
Info: 192 Carrer de Pau Claris (near the corner of Avinguda
Diagonal). Tel. 932174338. Open daily. Metro: Diagonal.

Elisabets €
This local restaurant serves breakfast and a very good fixed-
price lunch for around €11. You can also come here for drinks in
the evenings. Always crowded. *Info*: 2-4 Carrer Elisabets. Tel.
933175826. Closed Sat (lunch), Sun and most of Aug. Metro:
Catalunya.

El Xampanyet €
Xampanyerias are bars found in and around Barcelona serv-
ing *cava* (sparkling wine). This popular, blue-tiled bar is a great
place for a quick bite while visiting the Picasso Museum. *Info*: 22
Carrer Montcada. Tel. 933197003. Closed Mon, Sun (dinner) and
Aug. Metro: Jaume I.

Taverna Basca Irati €
Inexpensive *tapas* bar/restaurant. You'll find *tapas* on the bar
speared with toothpicks, and you're charged by the number of
toothpicks on your plate. The restaurant serves basic dishes such
as *chuletón* (beef chop). *Info*: 15 Carrer Cardenal Casañas (one
block off of La Rambla). Tel. 933023084. Closed Sun. Metro:
Liceu. www.sagardi.com.

Quimet y Quimet €
You can stand around the stainless-steel counter and munch on a
large selection of small sandwiches (*montaditos*) at this friendly,
family-owned bar. The walls are completely covered with wine
bottles and cans of specialty foods. *Info*: 25 Poeta Cabanyes. Tel.
934423142. Closed Sat (dinner) Sun and Aug. Metro: Paral.lel.

Barcelona: Tapas Bars

Head to the Drassanes metro stop at the southern end of La Rambla. All these eateries are near each other. Many are closed on Sunday and some in August.

Txikiteo at 7 Carrer de Josep Anselm Clavé. Take a look at the *tapas* on the long bar and take your pick with a glass of *txakolí* (a light and fruity Basque wine) while admiring the rustic stone, brick and timber walls. Sit at the bar. It's more fun. Ask about the frequent specials (like a glass of wine and three tapas for €3).

Bodega la Plata at 28 Carrer de la Mercè. People have been coming here to sit at tiny tables or stand at the marble-topped bar since the 1920s. It has a beautiful terrazzo floor and Mediterranean-tile walls. Try the house specialty: *sardinas* (deep-fried sardines, head and all) and a small glass of the house wine served from barrels along the wall. (Some of you may need more to drink before you can stomach the sardine heads!)

Across the street (17 Carrer de la Mercè) is **Tasca el Corral** (the place with the cured meats and onions and garlic hanging from the ceiling). This is the place to share a bottle of *sidra* (alcoholic cider). Try it, but be careful: It's stronger than it tastes. Notice how the waiter usually pours your drink with a grand gesture.

You'll find a wide selection of beer and *tapas* at **Cerveteca** at 25 Carrer d'en Gignàs.

Las Cuevas del Sorte at number 2 Carrer d'en Gignàs. This funky bar with cave-like décor is just the place to have a glass of *cava* (Spanish sparkling wine). You've had lots to drink by now, so head (no pun intended) to the fantastic tiled restrooms here.

Barcelona: Markets and Food Stores

Mercat de la Boqueria

Pass through the iron gateway to one of the largest, most interesting and colorful markets in Europe. You'll find everything from fresh produce to delicious snacks under its wrought iron-and-glass roof. Each stall in the market is numbered. *Info*: 91 La Rambla. Closed Sundays. Admission: Free. Metro: Plaça de Catalunya.

Mercat de Santa Caterina
Recently rebuilt, this is Barcelona's oldest marketplace. It features a mosaic roof, remains of a medieval convent, and colorful goods. *Info*: Between Avinguda Francesc Cambó and Carrer de Colomines. Metro: Jaume I.

J Murrià
A great place to stock up on local food specialties. The deli/grocery has been run by the same family since the early 1900s. *Info*: 85 Carrer de Roger Llúria. Tel. 932155789. Closed Sun. Metro: Passeig de Gràcia. www.muria.cat.

Bilbao
Mugarra €€€
This small restaurant serves modern Basque cuisine and is known for its fish dishes. You can also try the excellent *solomillo* (tenderloin). *Info*: 14. Tel. 944233914. Closed Sun and Aug. www.restaurantemugarra.com.

Harrobia €€
Friendly restaurant in the heart of the Old Town serving modern Basque dishes. Great salads. *Info*: 2 Calle Perro. Tel. 946790090. Closed Sun and Aug. www.harrobia.com.

Guggenheim Bilbao
A fantastic museum with two restaurants. **Nerua** (€€€) serves innovative Basque specialties. *Info*: Tel. 944000430. Closed Sun (dinner), Mon, and Tue (dinner). **Bistro Guggenheim** (€€) offers less formal fare. *Info*: Tel. 944239333. Closed Sun (dinner) and Mon. www.guggenheim.org/bilbao.

El Globo €-€€
Pinxtos (Basque *tapas*) are served at this popular eatery. Try the *txangurro* (seasoned crabmeat) and wash it down with a local wine. *Info*: 8 Diputacion. Tel. 944154221. Open daily.

Córdoba
La Almudaina €€-€€€
On the river in the Jewish Quarter, this is an elegant choice for lunch or dinner. The menu features both Spanish and French dishes. *Info*: 1 Campos Santos Mártires. Tel. 957474342. Closed Sun. www.restaurantealmudaina.com.

El Caballo Rojo €-€€€

An institution in this city and on the same street as the Mezquita (so it's a good choice for lunch), this restaurant serves local specialties like *rabo de toro* (oxtail stew) and *gazpacho*. *Tapas* and drinks at the bar downstairs (€), restaurant upstairs (€€€). *Info*: 28 Cardenal Herrero. Tel. 957475375. Open daily. www.elcaballorojo.com.

El Churrasco €€

Just northwest of the Mezquita in the Jewish Quarter is this attractive restaurant specializing in grilled dishes. Another good choice for lunch. *Info*: 16 Romero. Tel. 957290819. Open daily. Closed Aug. www.elchurrasco.com.

Café Gaudí €€

No, it wasn't designed by Gaudí, but the interior is done in a decidedly Gaudí style. The terrace is a great place to relax. The café is located between the train station and the Mezquita. Great breakfasts! *Info*: 22 Avenida del Gran Capitán. Tel. 957471736. Open daily.

Costa del Sol

Café de París €€€

Elegant café and restaurant featuring contemporary cuisine and creative desserts. Located in the La Malagueta district near the bullring. *Info*: 8 Calle Velez Málaga (Málaga). Tel. 952225043. Closed Sun and Mon. www.rcafedeparis.com.

Tapeo de Cervantes €€

Rave reviews for this small restaurant in the heart of Málaga where you can sample innovative and traditional *tapas*. Try the delicious *albóndigas de ternera* (veal meatballs). *Info*: 8 Calle Carcer (Málaga). Tel. 952609458. Closed Sun (lunch) and Mon. www.eltapeodecervantes.com

Matahambre €-€€

In Torremolinos, a city known for awful dining (Danish fast food anyone?), this friendly restaurant serves delicious salads and tapas. Truly a welcome dining surprise. Try the goat-cheese salad and wash it down with first-rate local wines. *Info*: 14 Calle las Mercedes (Torremolinos). Tel. 952381242. Open daily.

Pepa y Pepe €
If you're watching your euros, head to this dirt-cheap *tapas* bar where a glass of local wine will cost you less than two euro. *Info*: 9 Calle Calderería (Málaga). Open daily.

Granada

For *tapas* and drinks, try the Campo del Principe, where you will find many old-fashioned *tapas* bars.

Albahaca €€
Tiny restaurant serving Andalusian specialties (great *gazpacho*). It's located near the Santo Domingo church in a 100-year-old *mesón* (inn). The *menú del día* is a good bargain. *Info*: 17 Calle Verela. Tel. 958224923. Closed Sun, Mon and Aug.

Chikito €€-€€€
Popular restaurant and *tapas* bar. It's especially nice in fine weather, when you can sample *tapas* at tables on the square. *Info*: 9 Plaza del Campillo. Tel. 958223364. Closed Wed. Moderate (*tapas* bar)-Expensive (restaurant). www.restaurantechikito.com.

Mirador de Morayma €€
Large restaurant in the Albaicín neighborhood facing the Alhambra serving Spanish specialties. You can also dine outdoors. Convenient location for a lunch while visiting the Alhambra. *Info*: 2 Calle Pianista García Carillo. Tel. 958228290. Closed Sun (dinner). www.miradordemorayma.com.

La Oliva €€
This small food shop, wine store, and deli features the special-ties of Granada.You can also reserve a private group dinner with Francisco, the owner. A unique experience. *Info*: 9 Calle Rosario. Tel. 958225754. Closed Sat and Sun. www.laolivagourmet.com.

Parador de Granada €€
Located in the luxurious *parador* (state-owned hotel) within the grounds of the Alhambra, this restaurant serves Andalusian and Spanish specialties beneath a coffered ceiling. Try the excellent *gazpacho*. A great choice for lunch or an elegant dinner. *Info*: Real de la Alhambra. Tel. 958221440. Open daily.

Ibiza

El Olivo €€-€€€

Sit outdoors and watch the interesting parade of people while dining on local and international cuisine. Try the excellent *lomo de conejo* (fillet of rabbit) or *dorada a la plancha* (grilled dorada). *Info*: 7-9 Plaça de Vila. Tel. 971300680.

Trattoria del Mar €€

Dine at this restaurant on the Marina Botafoch while looking at the stunningly lit Old Town. The emphasis here is on Italian food, but you'll also find great seafood and local specialties. *Info*: On the Marina Botafoch. Tel. 971193934.

Madrid

Botín €€-€€€

Made famous in Ernest Hemingway's *The Sun Also Rises*. You'll eat in tiled, wood-beamed dining rooms in Madrid's (and allegedly, the world's) oldest restaurant. It's quite touristy, but the food, especially roast suckling pig (*cochinillo assado*), won't disappoint. *Info*: 17 Calle Cuchilleros. Tel. 913664217. Open daily. Metro: Puerta del Sol or La Latina. www.botin.es.

Casa Lucio €€-€€€

Spanish cuisine in an attractive setting (tiled floors, exposed brick walls and hams hanging from the ceiling). A specialty at this popular restaurant is *churrasco* (thick grilled steak). If it's good enough for King Juan Carlos and Bill Clinton, it should be good enough for you. *Info*: 35 Cava Baja. Tel. 913653252. Closed Sat. (lunch) and Aug. Metro: La Latina. www.casalucio.es.

Casa Paco €€-€€€

After a shot of red wine at the zinc-topped bar, you order steaks by weight in the tiled dining rooms. Grilled lamb and fish are also served. *Info*: 11 Plaza de Puerta Cerrada. Tel. 913663166. Closed Sun and Aug. Reservations required. Metro: La Latina.

El Bogavante de Almirante €€-€€€

This restaurant and bar (the Boga Bar) has an attractive deep red-and-black décor. It's located in a cave-like basement with a brick vaulted ceiling. The menu emphasizes seafood. If you're not in the mood for seafood, try the delicious *pato* (duck). *Info*: 11 Calle de Almirante. Tel. 915321850. Closed Sun (dinner) and part of Aug. Metro: Chueca.

Las Cuevas de Luis Candelas €€-€€€
Okay, so it's touristy with its strolling musicians and host dressed
like a bandit. But this "cave" off of the Plaza Mayor is the oldest
tavern in Madrid. *Tapas* and dining (especially barbecued meats).
Info: 1 Calle Cuchilleros. Tel. 913665428. Open daily. Metro:
Puerta del Sol or La Latina. www.lascuevasdeluiscandelas.com.

La Gamella €€-€€€
A little bit of the U.S. at this popular restaurant with good service
and innovative cuisine, where the American-born owner offers
a popular Sunday brunch. *Info*: 4 Calle de Alfonso XII. Tel.
915324509. Metro: Retiro. www.lagamella.com.

Bocaíto €€
Tapas and Spanish specialties at this tiled restaurant. Try the
plato combinado, a selection of many *tapas* served with a glass
of house wine (all for about €10). *Info*: 6 Calle de Libertad. Tel.
915321219. Closed Sat (lunch), Sun and most of Aug. Metro:
Banco de España or Chueca. www.bocaito.com.

El Mirador del Museo €€-€€€
International and Spanish dishes are served under the stars on the
top floor of the Museo Thyssen-Bornemisza. A truly unique expe-
rience. Good wine list. *Info*: 8 Paseo del Prado. Tel 914293984.
Open Jul and Aug. Reservations required. Metro: Banco de
España.

Da Cuchuffo €€
This popular restaurant serves delicious pasta dishes, pizza, and
Argentine steaks. Plenty of vegetarian options *Info*: 34 Juan
Álvarez Mendizábal. Tel. 915423203. Closed Mon, Tue, and Aug.
Metro: Plaza de España. www.cuchuffo.com.

Teatriz €€
An old theater remodeled into a wonderful restaurant with an
emphasis on Italian cuisine. Great food, a great experience, and
friendly service. It's known for its fantastic chocolate desserts.
Info: 15 Calle de Hermosilla (at Calle de Claudio Coello). Tel.
915775379. Closed part of Aug. Metro: Serrano.

La Taberna del Alabardero €-€€€
Near the Royal Palace and El Teatro Real, this small and charming taberna serves *tapas*, and has a wonderful restaurant in the back room serving Spanish and Basque cuisine. The pheasant (*faisán*) is great. *Info*: 6 Calle de Felipe V. Tel. 915472577. Open daily. Metro: Ópera. Inexpensive (*tapas*) – Moderate-Expensive (restaurant).

Casa Mingo €
You'll share sausages, roast chicken and salad at long tables with other diners at this *bodega* (tavern). Cider (*sidra*) is the drink of choice here. Not to be missed! *Info*: 34 Paseo de la Florida (across the street from Goya's tomb). Tel. 915477918. Open daily 11am-midnight. No reservations. No credit cards. Metro: Príncipe Pío (about a 10-minute walk from the metro stop).

Madrid: Market/ Food and Wine Stores
Mercado de San Miguel
This iron-and-glass building, built in 1915, is filled with fresh produce, meats and lots of stinky fish. *Info*: Plaza de San Miguel (off of Calle Mayor) near Plaza Mayor. Open daily. Metro: Ópera.

Chocolatería San Ginés
This 100-year-old *chocolateria* is where you can sample chocolate *churros y porras*. *Churros* are loops and *porras* are sticks of deep-fried batter which you dip in hot chocolate. *Info*: 5 Pasadizo de San Ginés (an alleyway off of Calle del Arenal). Tel. 913656546. Open Mon-Tue 6pm-7am, Wed-Sun 10am-7am. Metro: Ópera or Puerta del Sol.re behind the Plaza Santa Ana.

Mallorca
Open since the 1930s, this food and wine shop sells Spanish food specialties and a selection of Spanish wines. You can inexpensively sample the food at the *tapas* bar. There are several locations throughout the city. *Info*: 6 Calle de Serrano (at Calle de Columela). Tel. 915771859. Open daily. Metro: Retiro.

El Patrimonio Comunal Olivarero
Shop selling over 80 brands of high-quality Spanish olive oil. Take some home! *Info*: 1 Calle de Mejía Lequerica. Tel. 913080505. Closed Sun. Metro: Alonso Martínez.

Madrid: Tapas Bars

Head to the Plaza Santa Ana. All of these *tapas* bars are within walking distance of each other.

Casa Alberto at 18 Calle de las Huertas. Our favorite place for *tapas* in Madrid. This *taberna* and restaurant has been open since 1827. You'll have great *tapas* or main courses at reasonable prices, and the staff is exceptionally friendly. Why don't you stand at the bar and have *albóndigas de ternera* (veal meatballs)? They're fabulous! Down them with a glass of *vino tinto* (red wine).

Cervecería Alemana at 6 Plaza de Santa Ana. The best of the many *tapas* bars on the square, built in 1904 and modeled after a German beer hall (*Alemana* means "German" in Spanish). Have a beer. It'll be served in a white stein. Ernest Hemingway drank here, but that's really no big deal since he drank all over Madrid. Why don't you order *aceitunas* (olives), a popular snack? You'll be eating more later.

Another beer hall on the Plaza Santa Ana is **Cervecería Santa Ana** at number 10. Here you can have a plate of *jamón y queso* (cured ham and cheese).

Another *tapas* spot here is **La Moderna** at number 12. Try a glass of delicious Spanish wine and a cheese plate, for which this place is known.

Viva Madrid at 7 Calle de Manuel Fernández y González. It has fantastic tiled walls and an incredible carved ceiling. You come here to drink, and it's likely that the crowd will be lively.

At the tile bar **Taberna Toscana** (at 10-17 Calle de Manuel Fernández y González) you'll sit on stools and taste a wide selection of *tapas* under sausages hanging from the ceiling. Try the fantastic *ternera* (veal) dish swimming in a delicious sauce (with french fries). A specialty here (if you're up to it) is *morcilla* (blood sausage). Try it. It's an interesting choice. When in Spain…

Museo del Jamón

The "Museum of Ham" isn't really a museum, but a chain of delis serving and selling ham. It's not hard to notice the delis as you'll see hundreds of hams hanging from the ceiling. Try a glass of sherry and cured ham. There's a restaurant upstairs (where you will pay more). *Info*: 6 Carrera de San Jerónimo (near the Puerta del Sol). Tel. 915210346. Metro: Puerta del Sol. Other locations include the Plaza Mayor.

Pamplona

Alhambra €€€

Specialties of the Navarre region at this long-time favorite. Known for its selection of Spanish wines. *Info*: 7 Calle Bergamín. Tel. 948245007. Closed Sun.

Otano €€

This *tapas* bar and restaurant (near Plaza del Castillo) serves Navarre regional specialties. Try the delicious *solomillo* (tenderloin). *Info*: 5 Calle San Nicolás. Tel. 948225095. (There are many *tapas* bars on the Calle de Jarauta and Calle San Nicolás.)

Café Iruña €€

This attractive Art Deco café and restaurant is in the heart of the Old Town on Plaza del Castillo. Great for a drink, snack or *menú del día* (menu of the day). *Info*: 44 Plaza del Castillo. Tel. 948222064. Open daily. www.cafeiruna.com.

Ronda

Duquesa de Parcent €€-€€€

An elegant restaurant with upholstered chairs, handpainted walls and attentive service. For a light lunch, there are several soup and salad offerings or you can dine on delicious roast chicken with red peppers. There's a balcony overlooking the gorge and the New Bridge. *Info*: 12 Tenorio. Tel. 952871965.

Puerta Grande €€

This small restaurant is a short distance from the Plaza de España. Friendly service. Try the excellent *gazpacho*. *Info*: 10 Calle Nueva. Tel. 952879200.

Don Miguel €€

Touristy, but a great place for drinks overlooking the gorge and the New Bridge. It's located in the Hotel Don Miguel. *Info*: 4 Calle Villanueva (just off the Plaza de España). Tel. 952871090. Open daily. www.dmiguel.com. *129*

Restaurante Pedro Romero €€-€€€
It's appropriate that meat dishes dominate the menu at this
bullfight-themed restaurant. After all, it's located across from the
oldest bullring in Spain. Try the *chorizo* or the excellent *rabo de
toro* (oxtail). *Info*: 18 Virgen de la Paz. Tel. 952871110. Closed
Sun (dinner) and Mon Jun-Aug.

Tragabuches €€-€€€
A modern and inventive take on traditional Andalusian specialties such as *cochinillo asado* (grilled suckling pig). Many praise
the *menú de gustacíon* (a five-course taster's menu). *Info*: 1 Calle
José Aparicio (between Plaza de Toros and Plaza España). Tel.
952190291. Closed Sun. Reservations recommended.
www.tragabuches.com.

San Sebastián
Arzak €€€
Located in the childhood home of chef Juan Mari Arzak, this
celebrated restaurant is on the road heading to the border with
France. Traditional Basque specialties are served, often with
a French influence. It's a dining experience. Reservations are
required. *Info*: 21 Alto de Miracruz. Tel. 943285593. Closed Sun,
Mon, last half of June and Nov. www.arzak.es.

A Fuego Negro €€
Trendy *tapas* bar in the Old Town with a contemporary spin
on classic Basque dishes. *Info*: 31 Calle 31 de Agosto. Tel.
650135373. Closed Mon.

Casa Vallés €-€€
Restaurant and *tapas* bar, complete with hanging hams. It's near
the cathedral, and popular with locals. *Info*: 10 Reyes Católicos.
Tel. 943452210. Bar open daily. Restaurant closed Tue (dinner),
Wed, part of May. www.barvalles.com.

Santiago de Compostela
O Curro da Parra €€
This warm and friendly restaurant serves Galician cuisine, with
an emphasis on fresh, local ingredients. *Info*: 20 Rua Travesa. de
Castro. Tel. 981556059. www.ocurrodaparra.com.

O Beiro €-€€

You can taste Spanish wines and Galician specialties at this wine bar. *Info*: 3 Rua Raiña. Tel. 981581370. Open daily.

Casa Manolo €

Looking for a good value? This family-run restaurant serves Galician specialties with an Italian influence. You can only order two-course fixed-priced meals (but there are plenty of choices). Try the delicious cannelloni. *Info*: On Plaza Cervantes. Tel. 981582950. Closed Sun (dinner) and Jan.

Seville

Casa Román €-€€

A favorite *tapas* bar in the Barrio de Santa Cruz. You order at the counter in the front of the bar and enjoy a wide selection of *tapas*. *Info*: On the Plaza de los Venerables. Tel. 954228483. Open daily.

Egaña-Oriza €€€

On the edge of the Murillo Gardens, this celebrated restaurant serves the specialties of Seville with an emphasis on game dishes. *Info*: 41 San Fernando. Tel. 954227254.Closed Sun and Aug. Reservations required. www.restauranteoriza.com.

El Rinconcillo €-€€

One of the oldest bars in Seville. Your tab is often kept by chalk marks on the table. The food is straightforward and moderately priced. A great place to have a drink while visiting the Barrio de Santa Cruz. The tables are wine barrels. *Info*: 42 Gerona. Tel. 954223183. Closed Sun. www.elrinconcillo.es.

Enrique Becerra €€

Tapas bar and restaurant serving regional specialties with good service. Try the *huevos a la flamenca* (eggs baked with tomatoes, vegetables and sausage). Near the cathedral. *Info*: 2 Gamazo. Tel. 954213049. Closed Sun and Aug. www.enriquebecerra.com.

Vineria San Telmo €€

This cozy restaurant near the Alcazar gardens serves tasty *tapas*. Try the *atún a la plancha* (grilled tuna). Good quality for the price and a great wine selection. *Info*: 4 Paseo Catalina de Ribera. Tel. 954410600. Open daily. www.vineriasantelmo.com.

Seville: Tapas Bars

Head to the Triana neighborhood (from central Seville, cross the Guadalquivir River, on the bridge Puente Isabel II, also called Puente de Triana). Calle Betis, near the river, is home to *tapas* bars and *flamenco* clubs. Check out **La Albariza** at 6 Calle Betis. The specialty here is *puntillitos* (tiny fried squid). It's closed Sunday. A great spot for fantastic views of the city and the Guadalquivir River is the rooftop terrace at **El Faro de Triana** (restaurant and *tapas* bar) at the bridge Puente de Isabel II.

Toledo

Asador Adolfo €€-€€€

Just a short walk from the cathedral, the modern entry hides an intimate interior with painted decorations from the 1500s. Specialties of Toledo include *solomillo de cerdo* (pork loin with black truffles and wild mushrooms), and dishes accompanied with *flor de calabacín* (zucchini blossoms, usually in a saffron sauce). *Info*: 6 Calle Granada (at corner of Calle Hombre de Palo). Tel.925227321. Closed Sun (dinner), Mon and part of July.

La Perdiz €€

Located in the center of the old Jewish ghetto, this restaurant is named after Toledo's favorite dish of partridge (many versions of which are found on the menu). *Info*: 7 Calle de los Reyes Católicos. Tel. 925214658. Closed Sun (dinner) and part of Aug.

Hostel del Cardenal €€

This restaurant is located in the famous hotel of the same name. It's near the Bisagra Gate on the northern edge of the city walls. Local specialties, including roast suckling pig (*cochinillo asado*), served in a formal setting. Reservations required. *Info*: 24 Paseo de Recaredo. Tel. 925220862. Open daily.

Alfileritos 24 €-€€

This bar and restaurant serves *tapas* and local specialties. Try the *ciervo* (venison). Ample selection of wines by the glass and bottle. Helpful staff.. *Info*: 24 Alfileritos. Tel. 902106577. www.alfileritos24.com.

Valencia

In the Barrio Carmen, you can sample *tapas* in many places around the Plaza del Ayuntamiento and on Calle Alta.

Seu Xerea €€

This restaurant is frequented by locals and tourists who dine on Mediteranean and Asian cuisine. Try the interesting four choices on the *menú de tapas*. *Info*: 4 Calle Conde de Almodovar. Tel. 963924000. Closed Sat (lunch) and Sun. www.seuxerea.com.

El Timonel €€-€€€

The nautical décor is appropriate for this restaurant specializing in seafood (they also have good meat dishes). It's located just a few blocks from Valencia's Plaza de Toros, the largest bullring in Spain. *Info*: 13 Félix Pizcueta. Tel. 963526300. Closed Mon. www.eltimonel.com.

La Sucursal €€€

This restaurant in the Instituto Valenciano de Arte Moderno (IVAM) is known for its innovative Valencian dishes. It has an extensive list of regional wines. *Info*: 118 Calle Guillém Castro. Tel. 963746665. Reservations required. Closed Sat (lunch) and Sun. www.restaurantelasucursal.com.

Lisbon, Portugal

Mercado da Ribeira

Head to the most famous market in Lisbon. Locals have been buying everything from seafood to flowers here since the 1930s. Located in a building opposite the Cais do Sodré train station. Closed Sun.

Bocca €€€

Expect a warm welcome at this contemporary restaurant that opened in 2008. Try the innovative tasting menu which pairs modern Portuguese cuisine with interesting regional wine choices. *Info*: 87D Rua Rodrigo da Fonseca (off of Rua Braamcamp). Tel. 213808383. Closed Sun and Mon. www.bocca.pt.

Assinatura €€€

This restaurant with contemporary decor opened in 2010 and has a devoted following. You'll find creative takes on Portuguese specialties and attentive service. There's a good selection of Portuguese wines by the glass, and make sure you end your meal with the delicious assortment of Portuguese cheeses. *Info*: 19 Rua do Vale Pereiro (at Alexandre Hercuoano Av.). Tel. 213867696. Closed Mon (lunch), Sat (lunch), and Sun. www.assinatura.com.pt.

Casa da Comida €€€

This elegant restaurant is located in an 18th-century town-house with a lovely interior garden room. You'll dine on classic Portuguese dishes like *perdiz* (partridge) and *sargo* (sea bream). Excellent wine list and *queijos nacionais* (Portuguese cheese platter). Cordial staff. *Info*: 1 Travessa das Amoreiras (next to the Jardim das Amoreiras). Tel. 213885376. Closed Sun, Mon (lunch), and Sat (lunch). www.casadacomida.pt.

Solar dos Presuntos €€

Open for nearly 40 years, this lively and bustling restaurant serves traditional Portuguese cuisine with an emphasis on seafood to a mixture of locals and tourists. A good place to try the popular Portuguese specialty *bacalhau* (cod). It's said that the Portuguese have as many ways to prepare *bacalhau* as there are days in the year. *Info*: Rua das Portas de Santo Antão (near the Elevador do Lavra in the Baixa). Tel. 213424253. Closed Sun. www.solardospresuntos.com.

Wine Bar do Castelo €-€€

This popular wine shop and bar serves more than 150 Portuguese wines, and has a selection of cheese, cured meats, grilled sausages, and olives. It's located at the entrance to Saint George's Castle (Castelo de São Jorge). You'll learn about Portuguese wines and have fun doing it! Don't forget to try a glass of port. *Info*: 11-13 Rua Bartolomeu de Gusmão. Tel. 218879093. Closed Tue. Opens at 2pm.

Lighthouse €-€€

Casual dining (salads, sandwiches, hamburgers) at this cafe and bar in the Marina da Expo. Try the *chouriço*, a spicy smoked pork sausage. *Info*: Passeio de Neptuno, Marina da Expo, Parque das Naçoes. Tel. 919998800. www.lighthouse.pt.

Casa Pastéis de Belém €

No trip to Portugal would be complete without tasting the delicious *pastéis de Belém*, a custard tart. Expect to wait in line for a table, but it's worth it. *Info*: 84 Rua de Belém (Belém is less than 4 miles from Lisbon's city center). Tel. 213637423. Open daily 8am to 11pm (until midnight in summer). www.pasteisdebelem.pt.

Porto, Portugal

Mercado do Bolhão

You'll find everything from vegetables to flowers to seafood at this two-tier covered market in the center of town. Don't miss the entertaining wives of fishermen hawking the latest catch. *Info*: Rua Sá da Bandeira. Metro: Bolhão.

Vinologia

No trip to Porto would be complete without sampling the many varieties of port. This wine bar has an outstanding collection of ports by the glass or bottle, and the friendly staff will help you pair your port with cheese and chocolates (there is no restaurant). *Info*: 46 Rua de São João. Tel. 222052468. www.lamaisondesporto.com.

Cometa €€

This cozy restaurant is a modern take on a traditional Portuguese chop-house. Friendly service and reasonable prices. A good choice for a romantic dinner. *Info*: 87 Rua Tomás Gonzaga. Tel. 222008774. Closed Sun.

O Assador Típico €-€€

This restaurant (near the Museu Nacional de Soares dos Reis) specializes in grilled fish and meats. Try the *bacalhau assado na brasa* (grilled cod). The half-portion is usually enough for most diners. Good value and friendly service. *Info*: 22 Rua D. Manuel II. Tel. 222015149. Open daily. www.assadortipico.com.

Cufra €€

One of Porto's oldest seafood restaurants doesn't disappoint. Try the shellfish stew "à la Cufra." Tasty meat dishes are also available. *Info*: 2504 Avenida da Boavista. Tel. 226172715. Closed Mon. www.cufra.pt.

Shis €€-€€€

An evening at this modern restaurant, on Ourigo Beach at Foz do Douro, is a great experience. You can dine on everything from sushi to traditional Portuguese dishes. Attentive service and a sublime location. *Info*: Esplanada do Castelo/Praia do Ourigo/Foz do Douro. Tel. 226189593. Open daily. www.shisrestaurante.com.